100 ways AI can help...
Management Consultants

Joe Houghton

100 ways AI can help... Management Consultants
by Joe Houghton

First published in Ireland – September 2025
First edition – September 2025
© Copyright Joe Houghton 2025

Website:	https://www.houghton.consulting/books
Email:	joe@houghtonphoto.com
LinkedIn:	https://www.linkedin.com/in/joehoughton/

ISBN: 978-1-916579-17-0 (paperback)
ISBN: 978-1-916579-18-7 (hardback)

Dedication

This one is for all my Management Consulting students over the years – may your careers flourish and all your clients be happy ...

Table of Contents

Financial Analysis & Performance Management 77

Digital Transformation & Technology Consulting 98

Why read this book?

AI is reshaping our world – whether we like it or not. The surge in capabilities since ChatGPT 3 hit the public consciousness in November 2022 has been nothing short of astounding, and it shows no signs of letting up any time soon as I write this in Sept 2025.

What I want to do in this book is explore the way that tools like ChatGPT, Gemini and the other AI chat bots and tools can help Management Consultants do so many things quicker, faster and leveraging wider data sources than currently.

The idea is that you can copy and paste the prompts straight into whatever tool you prefer, and see immediate results.

Free vs paid tools

Most of the tools I've suggested have free and paid tiers, so you should be able to experiment with the prompts and approaches even using the free tools. At some point though, to get really thorough and in-depth research and analysis, you are probably going to have to take out paid subscription(s) to one or more of the tools. Especially in management consulting – your insights, analysis and recommendation have to better than the competitions, and just using thr free AI tools is not likely to help much with this...

Leaf through the pages and see just how many varied ideas there are...Come on in!

How I wrote the book...

One of my passions is technology, and I love all the gadgetry and tech around photography and computers in general. I started my professional career as a computer programmer, and have been scratching that itch ever since!

This book was written on a MacBook Pro with an M4 processor – one of the most significant jumps in computer power I've ever come across in my many years of using personal devices. It's set in 11 point Aptos font and edited in Microsoft Word.

My editing setup is to have the MacBook on the desk with a small stand and then I have it hooked up to a second screen mounted on the wall – a whopping 42" 4k TV that gives me loads of room for opening lots of windows as I do my research.

And for this book, given the recent emergence of a slew of new artificial intelligence tools, I've been playing with ChatGPT, Gemini and especially the newly updated version of Notion to help structure and offer up ideas for the materials within. The tools are amazing even in their early form – generating lists of points instantly that can then be reviewed and expanded upon.

There's still a lot of inaccuracies generated by the AI tools at the moment (Sept 2025) so anything they do return has to be read and edited very carefully, but using the tools definitely sped up the process of creating this little tome!

I hope you enjoy reading it as much as I enjoyed writing it – this book was a really fun exploration into emerging technologies whilst writing about a subject I love – doesn't get much better than that!

Joe Houghton
Dublin, Ireland, September 2025

Glossary of Tools

There are a number of different AI & other web-based tools mentioned in the 100 ideas – they are listed here in alphabetic together with the URL you can access them at. I tried to make sure that most of the tools have a free to access option so these ideas are as accessible as possible.

In most cases, where a specific chatbot tool is mentioned you can use exactly the same approach and prompts with any of the other chatbots. They'll all give slightly different responses, so the trick is to play with all of them and see which one provides you with the best answers to your specific needs

Of course. Here is a list of all the AI tools mentioned in the book, with their URLs and a brief description.

ChatGPT

https://chat.openai.com

A versatile conversational AI from OpenAI, used for a wide range of tasks including SWOT analysis, business model ideation, process mapping, and drafting reports.

Claude

https://claude.ai

An AI assistant from Anthropic, noted for its strong context handling and reasoning abilities, making it useful for scenario planning, drafting workflow automation suggestions, and developing integration plans.

Copilot

https://copilot.microsoft.com

Microsoft's AI assistant integrated into Office applications, enabling dynamic analysis within documents and spreadsheets for tasks like strategy formulation, cash flow forecasting, and creating compliance checklists

DeepSeek

https://DeepSeek.com

An AI tool with strong analytical capabilities, used for competitive differentiation analysis, evaluating product-market fit, and planning AI adoption by prototyping models.

Gamma

https://gamma.app

An AI tool that specializes in transforming structured content and bullet points into polished, visually compelling slide decks and presentations.

Grok

https://grok.x.ai

An AI from xAI capable of synthesizing information across various domains, used for generating Blue Ocean strategies, performing data analytics, and modelling employee attrition risk.

Notion AI

https://www.notion.so/product/ai

An AI assistant integrated within the Notion productivity workspace, used to build strategic roadmaps, create productivity dashboards, and organize findings from survey analysis.

Perplexity

https://www.perplexity.ai

An AI-powered search and summarization tool, harnessed to monitor industry trends, identify waste reduction opportunities, and research cybersecurity threats.

Qwen

https://qwen.alibaba.com

An AI from Alibaba, used for tasks like designing balanced scorecards, performing bottleneck analysis, creating synergy tracking dashboards, and calculating carbon footprints.

Business Strategy & Planning

1. AI-assisted SWOT analysis

Purpose

Using ChatGPT to facilitate SWOT brainstorming sessions allows consultants to pull together a wide range of perspectives without the need for long meetings. The AI can help you surface hidden strengths and weaknesses in your client's organisation and highlight opportunities and threats based on current market data. This technique helps structure strategic thinking and gives the team a starting framework for deeper analysis.

Unlike manual workshops, an AI-assisted SWOT can be updated quickly as new information comes in. It encourages participants to consider aspects they may have missed and provides a neutral sounding board that reduces bias. By embedding these insights into your planning process you create a living document that evolves with the project.

Benefits

- Encourages comprehensive analysis by listing strengths, weaknesses, opportunities and threats quickly
- Reduces meeting time by synthesising input from multiple sources
- Provides an impartial viewpoint that challenges groupthink
- Creates a structured record for later reference

How to do it

- Provide ChatGPT with company context and ask for a preliminary SWOT template
- Share the draft with stakeholders and invite comments or additional factors
- Refine the SWOT by prompting the AI for examples or industry-specific issues
- Translate the refined list into a strategic report or slide deck
- Review with the team and adjust the plan accordingly

Prompts

- Prompt: "You are a management consultant conducting a SWOT analysis for a mid-sized pharmaceutical company entering the digital health market. List potential strengths, weaknesses, opportunities and threats."
- Prompt: "Based on the following internal feedback and sales data, summarise the key opportunities we should prioritise in our SWOT."
- Chain: First ask ChatGPT to draft a general SWOT for the industry, then share your company's specific metrics and request a tailored SWOT based on those figures.

Tools to use

- ChatGPT (https://chat.openai.com)
- Notion AI for collaborative editing (https://www.notion.so/product/ai)
- Gamma for presenting the SWOT visually (https://gamma.app)

Metrics

- Number of unique SWOT factors generated
- Time saved compared with traditional brainstorming
- Stakeholder satisfaction scores

Cautions

- Ensure confidential data is anonymised before sharing with the AI
- Use the AI as a guide, not a substitute for expert judgement
- Cross-check AI-generated threats and opportunities with real market data

2. Trend analysis with Perplexity

Purpose

Perplexity's search and summarisation capabilities can be harnessed to monitor emerging industry trends. Management consultants often need to keep abreast of macroeconomic shifts, new technologies and competitor moves. Using an AI tool to compile and summarise recent articles, reports and news allows you to scan a wider set of sources in less time, which supports evidence-based strategic recommendations.

By feeding Perplexity with targeted queries you can collect insights on market size, consumer behaviour, regulatory changes and technological disruption. The service generates concise summaries and citations that you can cross-reference, helping you build a fact-driven narrative for your strategic plan. Because the summaries are generated on demand, you can refresh them regularly to keep your analysis current.

Benefits

- Provides up-to-date insights from a broad range of sources
- Saves hours of manual reading and note taking
- Helps identify early signals that may impact strategy
- Supports data-driven decision making with citations

How to do it

- Define the strategic question or industry segment you want to investigate
- Use Perplexity to perform a deep search using specific keywords and date ranges
- Review the generated summary and follow the citations to original sources for verification
- Extract key statistics and narratives to incorporate into your strategic analysis
- Regularly refresh the query to capture new developments

Prompts

- Prompt: "Summarise the latest trends in renewable energy adoption in Europe over the past 12 months with citations."
- Prompt: "What are analysts saying about the competitive landscape in the cloud computing market in 2025? Provide bullet points."
- Chain: Ask Perplexity to provide a high-level summary of market trends, then request deeper analysis on a specific competitor or technology mentioned in the summary.

Tools to use

- Perplexity (https://www.perplexity.ai)
- Excel or Google Sheets for organising extracted data
- Notion or OneNote for storing research notes

Metrics

- Number of relevant sources identified
- Time saved compared with manual research
- Accuracy and reliability of extracted data

Cautions

- Verify critical facts by consulting original sources
- Be aware of potential bias in the sources aggregated
- Avoid relying solely on AI summaries for regulatory or legal decisions

3. Scenario planning using Claude

Purpose

Scenario planning helps organisations prepare for multiple possible futures by envisioning different conditions and responses. Claude's context handling and long-form reasoning make it a useful partner for exploring alternative scenarios. Management consultants can outline key uncertainties – such as economic growth, customer adoption or regulatory change – and ask Claude to describe how these variables could interact.

The AI generates narrative descriptions of best-case, worst-case and middle-road scenarios. These narratives enable teams to consider potential opportunities and risks more holistically. In addition, Claude can help you identify trigger points that signal when to shift strategy. Incorporating scenario planning into your projects builds resilience into your recommendations.

Benefits

- Encourages proactive thinking about future uncertainties
- Helps clients understand the range of possible outcomes
- Identifies leading indicators and trigger events
- Facilitates strategic flexibility and contingency planning

How to do it

- Define the primary uncertainties affecting your client's business (e.g., regulatory changes, technology adoption)
- Ask Claude to generate detailed narratives for optimistic, pessimistic and neutral scenarios based on those uncertainties
- Review the scenarios with stakeholders and discuss their implications
- Develop contingency strategies and decision triggers aligned to each scenario
- Update the scenarios periodically as conditions evolve

Prompts

- Prompt: "Create three distinct scenarios for the adoption of autonomous vehicles in urban logistics by 2030, considering regulation, technology readiness and consumer acceptance."
- Prompt: "Given a global recession and tightening capital markets, describe how a mid-sized SaaS company's growth strategy might be affected."
- Chain: Start with Claude describing general macroeconomic scenarios, then ask follow-up questions about specific industries or business functions.

Tools to use

- Claude by Anthropic (https://claude.ai)
- Mind mapping tools like Miro (https://miro.com) for visualising scenarios
- Google Slides or PowerPoint to present the narratives

Metrics

- Number of distinct scenarios generated
- Stakeholder confidence in contingency plans
- Frequency of scenario updates

Cautions

- Avoid over-fitting scenarios to current assumptions
- Ensure the AI's narratives are grounded in plausible data
- Use scenarios as guides, not predictions

4. Blue Ocean strategy generator with Grok

Purpose

Blue Ocean strategy focuses on creating uncontested market space rather than competing head-to-head. Grok's ability to synthesise information across domains makes it well suited for identifying untapped opportunities. By prompting Grok to analyse adjacent industries, consumer pain points and emerging technologies, you can generate innovative value propositions that differentiate your client from competitors.

This technique encourages consultants to think creatively beyond incremental improvements. The AI can propose combinations of features or services that break traditional industry boundaries. Integrating these insights into strategic planning opens up new revenue streams and helps avoid price wars in saturated markets.

Benefits

- Stimulates creative thinking about uncontested market spaces
- Highlights unmet customer needs that competitors overlook
- Supports differentiation and avoids commoditisation
- Provides inspiration for new business models

How to do it

- Research the client's current market position and identify areas of intense competition
- Use Grok to explore adjacent industries and cross-domain innovations
- Generate a list of potential Blue Ocean opportunities with supporting rationale
- Evaluate each idea based on feasibility, strategic fit and customer value
- Develop a strategic roadmap to test and implement the most promising opportunities

Prompts

- Prompt: "Analyse the fitness industry and suggest Blue Ocean opportunities for a company specialising in wearable health devices."
- Prompt: "Identify unmet needs among gig-economy workers that could be served by new financial products."
- Chain: Ask Grok to list customer frustrations in an industry, then request innovative solutions that combine features from unrelated sectors.

Tools to use

- Grok from xAI (https://grok.x.ai)
- Business model canvas templates
- Customer interview notes and market data

Metrics

- Number of distinct value propositions generated
- Estimated market size of identified Blue Oceans
- Stakeholder buy-in to pursue new opportunities

Cautions

- Ensure ideas are validated through market research before investment
- Consider organisational capability to execute novel strategies
- Beware of over-reliance on AI for creativity; human judgment is still critical

5. Balanced scorecard design using Qwen

Purpose

The balanced scorecard translates strategy into a set of performance measures across financial, customer, internal process and learning perspectives. Qwen can assist consultants in designing scorecards by suggesting relevant metrics based on industry and strategic goals. By analysing your client's objectives and benchmarking data, Qwen proposes KPIs and targets that align with the strategy.

The AI also helps ensure balance across the four perspectives, preventing overemphasis on financial results at the expense of customer or learning dimensions. Using AI-generated suggestions as a starting point fosters alignment between leadership and operational teams, making the scorecard a more effective management tool.

Benefits

- Aligns metrics with strategic objectives
- Ensures balanced focus across financial and non-financial measures
- Reduces time spent on researching suitable KPIs
- Improves clarity for teams on what success looks like

How to do it

- Clarify the client's vision and strategic objectives
- Provide Qwen with industry context and strategic themes
- Review the AI's suggestions for KPIs under each perspective
- Customise targets and thresholds based on company data
- Implement the scorecard and establish reporting routines

Prompts

- Prompt: "Suggest balanced scorecard metrics for a retail bank aiming to improve customer loyalty and digital adoption."
- Prompt: "Given our objectives of reducing operational costs and boosting employee engagement, recommend KPIs across the four scorecard perspectives."
- Chain: Ask Qwen for generic scorecard metrics in your sector, then feed in your company's strategic priorities to refine the list.

Tools to use

- Qwen (https://qwen.alibaba.com)
- Excel or BI tools to build the scorecard dashboard
- Workshops with leadership to validate the measures

Metrics

- Number of relevant KPIs generated
- Time taken to design the scorecard
- Alignment between chosen KPIs and strategic goals

Cautions

- Avoid selecting too many metrics, which can dilute focus
- Ensure targets are realistic and based on reliable data
- Use the AI's suggestions as a starting point, not a final answer

6. Strategic roadmaps with Notion AI

Purpose

A strategic roadmap outlines milestones, initiatives and dependencies over time. Notion AI's task automation and templating features allow consultants to build interactive roadmaps that link narrative strategy to execution. By drafting the roadmap in Notion and using the AI to populate timelines and assign owners, you create a living document that the team can update as conditions change.

The AI can suggest logical sequencing of initiatives based on dependencies and resource constraints. Consultants can embed research notes, meeting summaries and KPIs directly within the roadmap, ensuring all stakeholders have context. This approach improves alignment and makes the plan more actionable.

Benefits

- Consolidates strategic initiatives, timelines and responsibilities in one place
- Automates creation of timelines and Gantt charts
- Facilitates collaboration and updates in real time
- Enhances transparency across teams

How to do it

- Create a new roadmap page in Notion and outline the strategic themes
- Use Notion AI to generate tasks, sub-tasks and suggested timelines based on the project goals
- Assign owners and due dates to each initiative
- Embed relevant documents, notes and KPIs within each roadmap item
- Review and adjust the roadmap regularly during project reviews

Prompts

- Prompt: "Generate a strategic roadmap for rolling out an enterprise resource planning system over 18 months with key milestones."
- Prompt: "Identify dependencies and critical paths for launching a new product line in Q3."
- Chain: Ask Notion AI to list all initiatives required for a digital transformation, then request a timeline and owner assignments for each initiative.

Tools to use

- Notion AI (https://www.notion.so/product/ai)
- Timeline and Kanban views within Notion
- Calendar integrations for due dates

Metrics

- Completion rate of roadmap milestones
- Frequency of roadmap updates
- Stakeholder engagement with the roadmap page

Cautions

- Ensure the roadmap remains flexible to accommodate changes
- Avoid overcomplicating timelines; keep them realistic
- Maintain version control if multiple stakeholders edit simultaneously

7. Competitive differentiation analysis using DeepSeek

Purpose

Differentiation is essential for standing out in crowded markets. DeepSeek's analytic capabilities can compare competitors across multiple dimensions such as pricing, features, customer satisfaction and brand positioning. By aggregating publicly available data and structured reports, DeepSeek helps consultants identify areas where a client can truly differentiate.

The AI can visualise comparative matrices and highlight gaps that represent opportunities. This approach helps refine value propositions and messaging. By understanding competitor strengths and weaknesses at a granular level, you can advise clients on where to invest to achieve sustainable advantage.

Benefits

- Aggregates disparate data sources for a comprehensive view
- Identifies differentiation opportunities across multiple dimensions
- Supports evidence-based positioning decisions
- Provides visual outputs that are easy to communicate

How to do it

- Gather competitor information such as product features, pricing and marketing materials
- Use DeepSeek to analyse and compare these attributes across competitors
- Identify areas where competitors are weak or where the market is underserved
- Develop differentiation strategies based on these insights
- Test the differentiation concepts with customer feedback or prototypes

Prompts

- Prompt: "Compare the feature sets and pricing models of the top five project management software vendors and identify gaps."
- Prompt: "What unique value propositions could a new entrant offer in the premium coffee shop market?"
- Chain: Ask DeepSeek to generate a competitive matrix, then request a list of differentiation strategies based on the identified gaps.

Tools to use

- DeepSeek (https://DeepSeek.com)
- Excel or BI tools for customised analysis
- Customer surveys to validate differentiation ideas

Metrics

- Number of differentiation opportunities identified
- Market feedback on proposed value propositions
- Time taken to generate comparative analysis

Cautions

- Data availability may vary across competitors
- Ensure ethical use of publicly available information
- Validate AI findings with qualitative market research

8. Strategy formulation conversation with Copilot

Purpose

Microsoft Copilot integrates with Office applications, enabling consultants to have dynamic strategy formulation conversations while working in documents or spreadsheets. By asking Copilot to explain the implications of different assumptions or to summarise large datasets, you can iterate strategic models more quickly. This interactive dialogue helps refine hypotheses and ensures that the analysis remains aligned to strategic objectives.

The AI can perform on-the-fly calculations, generate charts and highlight anomalies in data. It allows you to explore strategic options in Excel without needing to write complex formulas yourself. As a result, you spend less time on mechanics and more on interpretation and storytelling.

Benefits

- Speeds up data analysis and modelling within familiar Office tools
- Enables interactive exploration of "what-if" scenarios
- Reduces errors by automating formula writing and chart creation
- Frees up time for higher-level strategic thinking

How to do it

- Import or enter your data into Excel or Word
- Activate Copilot and describe the strategic analysis you want to perform
- Ask the AI to summarise trends, compute ratios or create visualisations
- Iterate by adjusting assumptions and requesting updated outputs
- Document insights and implications for strategy within your report

Prompts

- Prompt: "Analyse the last five years of revenue data and highlight which product lines are driving growth."
- Prompt: "Create a sensitivity analysis table showing how profit margins change with different cost of goods sold percentages."
- Chain: Request a summary of key financial trends, then ask Copilot to generate charts and discuss strategic implications for resource allocation.

Tools to use

- Microsoft Copilot (https://copilot.microsoft.com)
- Excel, Word and PowerPoint
- Power BI for more advanced visualisations

Metrics

- Time saved on modelling tasks
- Number of scenarios analysed
- Accuracy of AI-generated calculations compared to manual methods

Cautions

- Ensure the data fed into Copilot is accurate and clean
- Check formulas and outputs for reasonableness
- Be mindful of data security when using cloud-based AI features

9. Business model canvas ideation via ChatGPT

Purpose

The business model canvas provides a structured way to visualise how a company creates, delivers and captures value. ChatGPT can assist consultants in ideating and filling in each of the nine building blocks by asking probing questions and suggesting possibilities based on industry norms. This helps teams think through customer segments, value propositions, channels, revenue streams and cost structures in a coherent manner.

By using AI to prompt brainstorming, you can generate a wider range of options and challenge existing assumptions. The output can then be translated into a visual canvas using tools like Miro. This approach accelerates early-stage business design and ensures that no component of the model is overlooked.

Benefits

- Encourages comprehensive consideration of all nine business model elements
- Stimulates creative thinking and challenges assumptions
- Speeds up ideation sessions
- Produces a written record that can be refined and visualised later

How to do it

- Brief ChatGPT on the nature of the business and its goals
- Ask the AI to propose customer segments, value propositions and channels
- Iterate through each building block, prompting the AI for ideas and examples
- Review the AI's suggestions with the team and select the most promising
- Transfer the agreed elements into a business model canvas template

Prompts

- Prompt: "Draft a business model canvas for a subscription-based meal kit service targeting busy professionals."
- Prompt: "What revenue streams could a community solar project explore beyond selling electricity?"
- Chain: Ask ChatGPT to list potential customer segments, then follow up by requesting tailored value propositions for each segment.

Tools to use

- ChatGPT (https://chat.openai.com)
- Business model canvas templates (https://www.strategyzer.com/canvas/business-model-canvas)
- Miro or Canva for visualisation

Metrics

- Number of viable business model elements generated
- Diversity of ideas across segments and revenue streams
- Stakeholder engagement in the ideation session

Cautions

- Ensure the AI does not bias you toward generic business models
- Validate ideas with market research
- Be mindful of intellectual property when sharing competitive information

10. Growth strategy via Gamma

Purpose

Gamma specialises in creating polished slide decks from structured content. For growth strategy presentations, consultants can draft bullet points and data in plain text and let Gamma transform them into compelling visuals. The AI suggests layouts, icons and narrative flow that make the strategy easy to understand for executive audiences.

This tool is especially useful when time is limited but the message needs to be impactful. By combining the AI's design suggestions with your strategic content, you deliver professional-looking presentations without extensive design skills. Gamma also allows real-time edits, so you can iterate as feedback is received.

Benefits

- Accelerates the creation of professional presentations
- Improves clarity and visual appeal of strategy decks
- Enables non-designers to produce high-quality slides
- Allows quick iterations based on stakeholder feedback

How to do it

- Organise your growth strategy narrative into bullet points and data tables
- Upload the content to Gamma and select a suitable template
- Review the AI-generated slide deck and adjust layout or visuals as needed
- Incorporate charts, images and icons suggested by Gamma to enhance storytelling
- Export the final presentation and rehearse the delivery

Prompts

- Prompt: "Turn the following list of strategic growth initiatives and their timelines into a persuasive slide deck aimed at board members."
- Prompt: "Suggest visuals and colour schemes for a presentation on market expansion into Asia."
- Chain: Provide Gamma with an outline of the growth strategy, then ask for alternative narrative flows focusing separately on customer acquisition, product development and partnerships.

Tools to use

- Gamma (https://gamma.app)
- PowerPoint or Google Slides to finalise content
- Charting tools such as Power BI or Tableau for custom visuals

Metrics

- Time saved compared with manual slide creation
- Stakeholder comprehension and engagement during presentation
- Number of iterations required before approval

Cautions

- Ensure the AI's design choices align with corporate branding
- Review slides for accuracy and consistency
- Avoid overloading slides with too much text; keep messages concise

Market Research & Competitive Analysis

11. Web scraping competitor pricing using Python & ChatGPT

Purpose

Understanding competitor pricing helps consultants benchmark a client's offerings. With Python scripting and assistance from ChatGPT's code generation capabilities, you can automate the extraction of pricing data from competitor websites. The AI can help write or debug a script that collects product names, prices and features from multiple online sources.

Automating this task not only reduces manual effort but also makes it feasible to track price changes over time. Once the data is collected, you can analyse pricing trends, identify premium and budget segments and recommend strategic adjustments to your client's pricing strategy.

Benefits

- Automates a repetitive data collection task
- Provides up-to-date competitor pricing information
- Supports data-driven pricing recommendations
- Enables monitoring of price changes over time

How to do it

- Identify competitor websites and the products or services to monitor
- Use ChatGPT to generate or review a Python web scraping script using libraries like BeautifulSoup or Scrapy
- Run the script to collect pricing data and store it in a structured format such as CSV
- Analyse the data using Excel or a BI tool to detect patterns and anomalies
- Present your findings and pricing recommendations to the client

Prompts

- Prompt: "Write a Python script using BeautifulSoup to scrape product names and prices from the first two pages of an online retailer's laptop category."
- Prompt: "How can I modify this script to handle dynamic pages powered by JavaScript?"
- Chain: First ask ChatGPT to produce a basic scraping script, then request help optimising it for multiple competitor sites and data formats.

Tools to use

- ChatGPT (https://chat.openai.com)
- Python with BeautifulSoup, Requests or Selenium
- Excel or Pandas for data analysis

Metrics

- Number of competitor products tracked
- Frequency of price updates collected
- Accuracy of scraped data compared to manual checks

Cautions

- Respect website terms of service and robots.txt rules
- Be mindful of legal restrictions around scraping
- Validate data to ensure scraping errors do not skew analysis

12. Customer sentiment analysis from social media using Copilot & Excel

Purpose

Analysing social media sentiment offers insight into customer perceptions of your client and their competitors. With Microsoft Copilot integrated into Excel, consultants can import social media data via APIs and use AI functions to classify posts as positive, negative or neutral. This approach enables quick aggregation of opinions across platforms such as Twitter and Facebook.

By examining trending themes and sentiment patterns, you can identify strengths to build upon and issues requiring attention. The data also feeds into marketing strategies and product improvements. Automating sentiment classification speeds up analysis and reduces the subjective bias of manual review.

Benefits

- Provides real-time feedback from customers
- Highlights emerging issues before they become crises
- Informs marketing and product development strategies
- Reduces manual effort in classifying large volumes of posts

How to do it

- Access social media data through APIs or third-party tools and import into Excel
- Enable Copilot and ask it to classify each comment or post as positive, neutral or negative
- Use pivot tables or charts to summarise sentiment by topic, time period or competitor
- Identify recurring themes that warrant further investigation
- Share the insights with marketing or product teams and track follow-up actions

Prompts

- Prompt: "Classify these 500 Twitter mentions of our brand into positive, negative and neutral categories and highlight the most common complaints."
- Prompt: "Create a chart showing how sentiment towards our latest product launch has evolved over the past month."
- Chain: Ask Copilot to summarise overall sentiment, then request a breakdown by feature or keyword mentioned in the posts.

Tools to use

- Microsoft Copilot (https://copilot.microsoft.com)
- Excel with data connectors
- Social media APIs or tools like Brandwatch

Metrics

- Volume of posts analysed
- Sentiment distribution across positive, neutral and negative categories
- Changes in sentiment after marketing campaigns

Cautions

- Ensure compliance with data privacy regulations when collecting social media data
- Beware of sarcasm or idiomatic expressions that AI might misclassify
- Complement AI findings with human review for nuanced insights

13. Market segmentation clustering with Claude & ChatGPT

Purpose

Effective marketing and product development rely on understanding distinct customer segments. Claude and ChatGPT can assist by analysing demographic, behavioural and psychographic data to propose meaningful clusters. The AI can suggest segmentation criteria, run clustering algorithms via code generation and interpret the resulting segments.

This approach helps consultants identify underserved niches and tailor strategies to each segment. Combining AI-generated clusters with qualitative insights ensures that the segments are both statistically sound and practically relevant. The result is a more targeted allocation of marketing resources and better customer satisfaction.

Benefits

- Reveals hidden patterns in customer data
- Supports personalised marketing and product design
- Increases marketing ROI by targeting the right segments
- Combines quantitative clustering with qualitative interpretation

How to do it

- Collect customer data from CRM systems or surveys, ensuring it is anonymised
- Use ChatGPT to generate code for clustering algorithms in Python (e.g., K-means, DBSCAN)
- Run the clustering algorithm and ask Claude to interpret the characteristics of each cluster
- Validate the clusters with business stakeholders and refine as needed
- Design segment-specific marketing and product initiatives based on the insights

Prompts

- Prompt: "Given a dataset with age, spending score and product preferences, write Python code to perform K-means clustering and describe the resulting clusters."
- Prompt: "Interpret these three customer clusters in terms of lifestyle and buying motivations."
- Chain: Ask ChatGPT to prepare the clustering code, then request Claude to summarise the profiles of each cluster and suggest marketing messages.

Tools to use

- ChatGPT and Claude (https://openai.com and https://claude.ai)
- Python with scikit-learn library
- Visualisation tools such as Tableau or Power BI

Metrics

- Number of clusters identified
- Distinctive features and behaviours of each segment
- Conversion rates after segment-targeted campaigns

Cautions

- Ensure data privacy and compliance when handling personal information
- Avoid over-segmentation which can lead to fragmented messaging
- Validate AI-suggested segments with real customer feedback

14. Trend forecasting via Perplexity using aggregator news summarisation

Purpose

Accurate forecasting requires staying abreast of news across multiple industries and regions. Perplexity's ability to summarise news from diverse sources helps consultants detect patterns and forecast trends. By aggregating articles and reports around specific keywords or sectors, you can identify common themes, emerging technologies and shifting consumer behaviours.

The AI summarises articles into digestible bullet points and highlights key statistics. Consultants can then interpret these signals in the context of their client's business and build forecasting models. Regularly scanning aggregated news ensures that your trend analyses remain current and helps pre-empt changes in the competitive landscape.

Benefits

- Accesses a wide range of news sources quickly
- Condenses large volumes of information into key insights
- Supports early detection of emerging trends
- Enhances the quality of forecasting models

How to do it

- Identify the focus areas or sectors relevant to your client
- Use Perplexity to search and summarise recent news articles on these topics
- Compile the summaries into a repository or dashboard
- Analyse recurring themes and correlations with other data sources
- Incorporate the insights into forecasting models or advisory reports

Prompts

- Prompt: "Summarise the top news stories about artificial intelligence ethics and regulation from the past quarter."
- Prompt: "What emerging consumer trends are noted in recent articles about sustainable fashion?"
- Chain: Ask Perplexity to list key points from a set of articles, then request a synthesis that relates those points to your client's industry.

Tools to use

- Perplexity (https://www.perplexity.ai)
- RSS feed readers or API connectors
- Excel or Notion for organising summaries

Metrics

- Number of articles summarised
- Relevance of the identified trends to the client's strategy
- Accuracy of forecasts informed by these insights

Cautions

- Beware of misinformation and verify sources
- Avoid confirmation bias by scanning a diverse range of publications
- Regularly update the trend analysis to reflect new information

15. Competitor benchmarking reports summarised by Notion AI

Purpose

Comprehensive competitor benchmarking often results in lengthy reports. Notion AI can condense these reports into concise summaries that highlight critical findings. Consultants can feed full benchmarking documents into Notion and ask the AI to extract key metrics, strengths, weaknesses and strategic differences across competitors.

Summarised insights save time for busy executives and make the information more accessible. The AI can also generate comparative tables and highlight recommendations. This approach streamlines the preparation of competitor briefings and keeps the focus on actionable intelligence rather than dense detail.

Benefits

- Transforms long reports into digestible summaries
- Highlights the most relevant competitive insights
- Supports quick decision making by executives
- Reduces manual summarisation effort

How to do it

- Collect detailed benchmarking reports or competitor analyses
- Import the documents into a Notion page
- Use Notion AI to summarise each report into key metrics, strengths and weaknesses
- Create a comparison table within Notion to juxtapose competitors on critical dimensions
- Review the summary with stakeholders and identify strategic implications

Prompts

- Prompt: "Summarise this 30-page competitor analysis into a one-page brief highlighting market share, growth rate and product differentiation."
- Prompt: "Generate a table comparing the pricing, features and customer satisfaction scores of the top three competitors in the SaaS sector."
- Chain: Ask Notion AI to summarise individual reports, then request a synthesis across all reports that highlights overall industry trends.

Tools to use

- Notion AI (https://www.notion.so/product/ai)
- Excel or Google Sheets for further analysis
- Presentation tools for sharing insights

Metrics

- Reduction in report length
- Time saved in reading and summarising
- Stakeholder comprehension of competitor dynamics

Cautions

- Ensure summarisation preserves nuance and avoids misinterpretation
- Cross-check the AI's summaries against original reports
- Be cautious about sharing proprietary competitor information

16. Survey design using Qwen

Purpose

Good market research depends on well-designed surveys. Qwen can help consultants craft survey questions that are clear, unbiased and targeted to specific segments. By providing context about the research objectives and audience, you can ask the AI to suggest question formats, response scales and branching logic.

The AI may also highlight potential biases or leading language, helping improve survey quality. Thoughtfully designed surveys lead to better response rates and more reliable data, which in turn enhances the quality of market insights and recommendations for clients.

Benefits

- Improves clarity and neutrality of survey questions
- Tailors surveys to specific audience segments
- Helps design logical flow and branching
- Increases response rates and data reliability

How to do it

- Define the research objectives and target audience for the survey
- Provide Qwen with this context and request suggestions for question wording and response options
- Review and refine the AI-generated questions to ensure they align with your goals
- Use survey software to implement branching or skip logic as suggested
- Pilot the survey with a small group and iterate based on feedback

Prompts

- Prompt: "Draft a set of survey questions to understand customer satisfaction with online banking services, using a 5-point Likert scale."
- Prompt: "How can I ask about price sensitivity without leading the respondent?"
- Chain: Ask Qwen for general customer satisfaction questions, then request adaptations for different age groups or geographic regions.

Tools to use

- Qwen (https://qwen.alibaba.com)
- Survey platforms like SurveyMonkey or Qualtrics
- Excel or Python for analysing responses

Metrics

- Completion rate of surveys
- Response quality (e.g., completeness and variance)
- Number of follow-up questions clarified during pilots

Cautions

- Avoid leading or ambiguous questions
- Ensure the survey length does not discourage respondents
- Comply with data privacy regulations when collecting responses

17. Product-market fit evaluation using DeepSeek

Purpose

Assessing product-market fit requires understanding customer needs, value perception and competitive offerings. DeepSeek can analyse feedback from reviews, surveys and support tickets to gauge how well a product meets market expectations. The AI identifies recurring themes and calculates sentiment scores, providing a quantitative and qualitative view of fit.

Consultants can use these insights to recommend product adjustments, repositioning or new feature development. Evaluating product-market fit early helps avoid costly missteps and informs resource allocation. Continuous monitoring ensures the product evolves with market demands.

Benefits

- Aggregates feedback from multiple channels
- Provides quantitative indicators of fit through sentiment and usage metrics
- Highlights specific features that delight or frustrate customers
- Informs strategic product decisions

How to do it

- Collect qualitative data from reviews, surveys and support logs
- Use DeepSeek to perform sentiment analysis and topic modelling on the data
- Identify strengths and weaknesses in the product based on customer feedback
- Compare your client's product fit with competitor offerings using the same method
- Develop recommendations for improving product-market fit

Prompts

- Prompt: "Analyse customer reviews of our mobile app and identify the top three features users love and the top three pain points."
- Prompt: "Compare sentiment scores for feature A versus feature B across all feedback channels."
- Chain: Ask DeepSeek to summarise product fit issues, then request specific recommendations for features or messaging to improve fit.

Tools to use

- DeepSeek (https://DeepSeek.com)
- Python for custom analytics
- Data visualisation tools to present findings

Metrics

- Overall sentiment score
- Net Promoter Score (NPS)
- Frequency of specific feature mentions

Cautions

- Feedback may be skewed towards vocal customers; seek a representative sample
- Complement quantitative analysis with qualitative interviews
- Be wary of over-fitting to current feedback if the market is rapidly evolving

18. Social listening via Grok's summarisation

Purpose

Social listening involves monitoring conversations across social platforms to understand public sentiment and emerging topics. Grok's summarisation capabilities can process large volumes of social data and highlight key themes, influencers and trending discussions. For management consultants, this provides early insight into reputational risks and opportunities for clients.

By turning unstructured posts into concise summaries, the AI helps you prioritise issues worth addressing. It can also identify potential brand advocates or detractors. Regular social listening informs communication strategies, crisis management plans and product development.

Benefits

- Detects emerging issues before they become mainstream
- Identifies influential voices and communities
- Supports proactive reputation management
- Provides data for refining marketing and communication strategies

How to do it

- Set up social listening feeds across relevant platforms and keywords
- Use Grok to summarise daily or weekly data into themes and sentiment trends
- Identify top influencers discussing the client or industry topics
- Share insights with marketing, communications and product teams
- Track changes over time to measure the impact of interventions

Prompts

- Prompt: "Summarise discussions on LinkedIn about remote work policies within the past two weeks, focusing on employee concerns."
- Prompt: "Identify key influencers and hashtags associated with our recent product launch on Instagram."
- Chain: Ask Grok to summarise the sentiment around a specific campaign, then request recommendations on how to respond to negative feedback.

Tools to use

- Grok (https://grok.x.ai)
- Social listening platforms like Sprout Social or Hootsuite
- Excel or BI tools to track metrics over time

Metrics

- Volume of mentions per topic
- Sentiment score trends over time
- Engagement rates of identified influencers

Cautions

- Ensure ethical use of public data and respect privacy settings
- Avoid reacting to every negative mention; focus on patterns
- Cross-check AI summaries with manual review to catch nuance

19. Economic indicator analysis using ChatGPT and FRED data

Purpose

Economic indicators such as GDP growth, inflation and unemployment influence strategic decisions. By using ChatGPT to interpret data from sources like the Federal Reserve Economic Database (FRED), consultants can quickly extract trends and correlations. The AI can pull data via API queries or spreadsheets and help explain what the numbers mean for your client's industry.

This approach simplifies complex macroeconomic data and ties it directly to strategic questions. It enables consultants to provide timely insights in client meetings and ensures that recommendations consider broader economic conditions.

Benefits

- Transforms macroeconomic data into actionable insights
- Provides context for strategic planning and forecasting
- Automates data retrieval and reduces manual analysis
- Enhances credibility by grounding advice in economic evidence

How to do it

- Identify the economic indicators relevant to your client's business
- Use Python or a data connector to retrieve FRED data into a spreadsheet
- Ask ChatGPT to summarise trends and explain the potential impact on the client's sector
- Create charts and dashboards to visualise the data for stakeholders
- Incorporate the insights into financial models and strategic discussions

Prompts

- Prompt: "Retrieve and summarise the trend of the US Consumer Price Index over the past 10 years and discuss implications for a consumer goods company."
- Prompt: "Explain how changes in interest rates might affect capital investment decisions for a manufacturing firm."
- Chain: Request ChatGPT to provide historical data on unemployment, then ask for correlations with discretionary spending in the retail sector.

Tools to use

- ChatGPT (https://chat.openai.com)
- FRED API (https://fred.stlouisfed.org)
- Excel or BI tools for analysis

Metrics

- Number of economic indicators analysed
- Clarity of interpretations provided
- Improvement in forecasting accuracy when economic context is included

Cautions

- Macroeconomic data may lag; supplement with real-time indicators where possible
- Avoid over-interpreting short-term fluctuations
- Cross-validate AI interpretations with expert economic analysis

20. Net Promoter Score analysis with Notion & ChatGPT

Purpose

Net Promoter Score (NPS) is a widely used metric to gauge customer loyalty. Notion provides a flexible database to collect survey responses, while ChatGPT can analyse open-ended feedback and group comments into themes. By combining these tools, consultants can go beyond the numeric NPS to understand the reasons behind customer advocacy or dissatisfaction.

This deeper understanding helps prioritise improvements that will have the greatest impact on loyalty. The AI can also suggest follow-up questions or interventions for detractors. Regular analysis ensures that client organisations remain responsive to customer needs and can track the impact of changes over time.

Benefits

- Combines quantitative and qualitative analysis of NPS
- Identifies root causes behind promoters and detractors
- Supports targeted action plans to improve loyalty
- Automates categorisation of free-text feedback

How to do it

- Set up a Notion database to collect NPS survey responses and comments
- Calculate the NPS score by subtracting the percentage of detractors from promoters
- Use ChatGPT to analyse comments and categorise them into themes such as service quality, product features or pricing
- Prioritise themes based on frequency and impact on loyalty
- Design and implement interventions to address key pain points and track NPS over time

Prompts

- Prompt: "Analyse the following customer comments and classify them into themes that explain why they are promoters or detractors."
- Prompt: "Suggest actions that could convert detractors into promoters based on these themes."
- Chain: Ask ChatGPT to summarise detractor comments, then follow up by requesting actionable recommendations for improvement.

Tools to use

- Notion (https://www.notion.so)
- ChatGPT (https://chat.openai.com)
- Survey tools to collect NPS responses

Metrics

- NPS score
- Number of comments analysed and categorised
- Impact of interventions on subsequent NPS surveys

Cautions

- Ensure anonymity and confidentiality in survey responses
- Avoid overreacting to outlier comments; focus on patterns
- Combine NPS with other customer experience metrics for a holistic view

Operational Efficiency & Process Optimisation

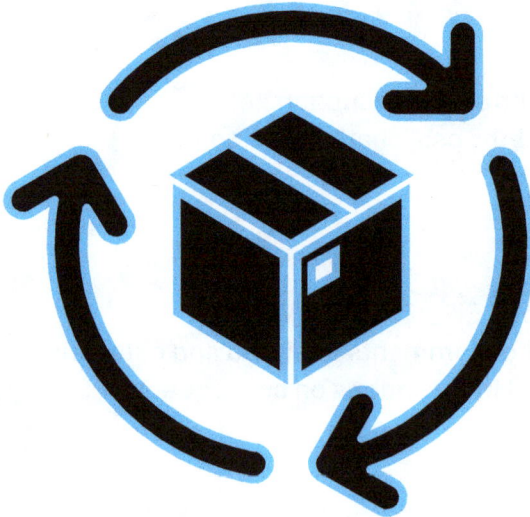

21. Process mapping with ChatGPT

Purpose

Creating clear process maps from messy or unstructured procedure descriptions is a crucial first step for consultants involved in operational efficiency projects. Often, consultants are presented with a variety of written materials, such as standard operating procedures (SOPs), emails, or informal notes, which lack consistency and clarity. By distilling these sources into coherent process maps, consultants can visualise current workflows and identify the main steps involved.

This visualisation not only brings structure to complex or ambiguous processes but also helps to highlight redundancies, bottlenecks, and unnecessary hand-offs. A well-constructed process map enables stakeholders from different backgrounds to quickly understand the existing workflow and align on what is actually happening versus what is intended. This alignment is essential before moving forward with any process optimisation or improvement initiatives.

Clear process maps also serve as the foundation for advanced analysis techniques, such as Lean or Six Sigma. By establishing a visual baseline, consultants can use these maps to pinpoint areas for improvement, track changes over time, and measure the impact of interventions. Ultimately, transforming messy procedure descriptions into clear process visualisations is a vital part of driving meaningful and sustainable operational improvements.

Benefits

- Fast creation of draft process diagrams without specialist software
- Highlights redundancies and unnecessary hand-offs
- Enables stakeholders to align on current state quickly
- Forms a baseline for lean or Six Sigma analysis

How to do it

1. Gather written descriptions or SOPs from the client
2. Use ChatGPT to summarise the steps in a linear sequence
3. Ask the AI to identify inputs, outputs and decision points
4. Translate the summary into a simple flowchart or swim lane diagram
5. Review with subject matter experts and refine the map

Prompts

- 'Summarise the key steps in the attached procedure text'
- 'Identify decision points and outcomes in this workflow description'
- 'Rewrite the process description as bullet points that can be used for a flowchart'
- Chain: 'List the steps in this process' → 'Now suggest how to group these steps into phases'

Tools to use

- ChatGPT
- Lucidchart
- Notion AI

Metrics

- Number of redundancies identified
- Time taken to produce the first map versus manual mapping
- Stakeholder satisfaction with the accuracy of the map

Cautions

- Verify the AI's interpretation with process owners
- Ensure sensitive process details are anonymised before sharing with cloud services
- Use visualisation tools to clarify sequence and parallel activities

22. Lean Six Sigma data analysis using Copilot & Excel

Purpose

Analysing operational data is essential for identifying sources of waste, inefficiency, and variation within business processes. By systematically reviewing cycle times, defect counts, and other performance metrics, organisations gain valuable insights that drive continuous improvement.

This data-driven approach is at the core of Lean Six Sigma methodologies, ensuring that process refinements are based on evidence rather than assumption or opinion. Incorporating AI tools can significantly accelerate the process of analysing large datasets, automating complex statistical calculations and highlighting trends or outliers that may otherwise be overlooked.

Leveraging AI not only speeds up the identification of root causes but also supports more accurate and reliable decision-making. As a result, teams can focus their efforts on interpreting results and implementing effective solutions, ultimately increasing the overall efficiency and quality of operations.

Benefits

- Automates descriptive statistics and control chart creation
- Helps prioritise process issues based on data rather than opinion
- Frees up consultant time to interpret results and engage stakeholders
- Improves accuracy by reducing manual formula errors

How to do it

1. Collect process performance data (cycle times, defect counts)
2. Use Copilot in Excel to generate summary statistics and

identify outliers
3. Ask the AI to produce Pareto charts or histograms automatically
4. Interpret the results to pinpoint high-impact issues
5. Propose targeted improvements based on the analysis

Prompts

- 'Create a control chart from this defect data and identify if the process is in control'
- 'Generate a Pareto chart ranking the causes of delays by frequency'
- 'What does the distribution of cycle times suggest about process capability?'
- Chain: 'Summarise the mean, median and standard deviation of this data' → 'Recommend which process steps should be addressed first'

Tools to use

- Microsoft Copilot
- Excel
- Minitab

Metrics

- Reduction in process variation after improvements
- Cycle time or defect rate reduction
- Percentage of stakeholders adopting data-driven decisions

Cautions

- Check that AI-generated charts follow accepted statistical rules
- Don't rely solely on statistical significance – consider practical impact
- Protect confidential operational data when using cloud AI

23. Workflow automation suggestions with Claude

Purpose

To maximise efficiency, it is important to systematically identify manual tasks that are suitable for automation. These often include repetitive processes, data entry, or rule-based activities that consume valuable employee time.

Consultants play a crucial role in guiding organisations through the selection process, helping clients evaluate where robotic process automation (RPA) or simple automation scripts can deliver the greatest value. Their expertise ensures that automation efforts align with business strategy and operational goals.

Artificial intelligence further streamlines this process by scanning job descriptions and workflow documentation to highlight candidate tasks for automation. This approach allows organisations to quickly pinpoint areas where automation can improve productivity and reduce errors.

Benefits

- Rapidly surfaces repetitive actions across departments
- Supports business cases for robotic process automation
- Improves employee satisfaction by removing mundane work
- Creates a backlog of automation opportunities aligned with strategy

How to do it

1. Collect descriptions of daily tasks from different teams
2. Prompt Claude to identify high-volume, rules-based activities
3. Evaluate feasibility by asking AI about system integrations needed
4. Prioritise tasks based on expected time saved and

complexity

5. Present recommendations to leadership with estimated ROI

Prompts

- 'Review these task descriptions and highlight activities that could be automated'
- 'Estimate the potential time savings if these tasks were automated'
- 'What system integrations would be required to automate invoice approvals?'
- Chain: 'List manual steps in our accounts payable process' → 'Suggest which steps a bot could handle and what remains manual'

Tools to use

- Claude
- UiPath
- Power Automate

Metrics

- Number of candidate automation tasks identified
- Estimated hours saved per month
- Implementation success rate for recommended automations

Cautions

- Validate automation suitability with IT and compliance
- Avoid over-automating tasks that require human judgement
- Ensure change management accompanies new bots

24. LEAN - waste reduction identification via Perplexity

Purpose

Leveraging artificial intelligence offers a powerful way to analyse operations logs and bring to light activities that do not contribute value to the business. By automating the review process, AI can efficiently identify patterns and spot inefficiencies that might otherwise go unnoticed.

Using tools like Perplexity, organisations can take advantage of advanced web search capabilities to gather summaries of lean best practices relevant to their industry. This enables teams to benchmark their current procedures against established standards and recommendations from external sources.

Comparing these findings with existing workflows helps highlight gaps and opportunities for improvement. With a clear understanding of non-value-added activities, companies are better equipped to implement targeted changes, reduce waste, and support ongoing continuous improvement initiatives.

Benefits

- Helps uncover hidden inefficiencies and waiting times
- Provides benchmarking data from external sources
- Supports continuous improvement initiatives with evidence
- Encourages cross-functional dialogue about waste

How to do it

1. Gather logs or daily activity reports from the client
2. Ask Perplexity to summarise lean best practices in similar industries
3. Compare current activities with recommended practices to identify gaps
4. Categorise identified wastes (e.g., overproduction, transport, waiting)

5. Prioritise quick wins and develop action plans

Prompts

- 'What are common forms of waste in manufacturing according to lean principles?'
- 'Compare our procedure with industry best practices and identify mismatches'
- 'Summarise the top three sources of delay in this activity log'
- Chain: 'List all instances where tasks wait for approvals' → 'How could technology reduce these waiting times?'

Tools to use

- Perplexity
- Lean literature databases
- Notion

Metrics

- Number of waste sources identified and eliminated
- Time or cost savings realised
- Employee feedback on process changes

Cautions

- AI may not understand subtle contextual reasons for certain steps
- Ensure recommended changes do not violate regulatory requirements
- Balance efficiency gains with quality and safety considerations

25. Supplier performance analysis with ChatGPT

Purpose

Analyse supplier scorecards and unstructured comments to find performance trends. AI can help consultants summarise narrative feedback and highlight areas for negotiation.

As management consultants often tackle a wide variety of operational efficiency & process optimisation challenges, AI helps translate disparate data and perspectives into structured insights. By tapping into the language models' ability to synthesise information, consultants can shorten research cycles and spend more time on high-value analysis and client engagement.

Benefits

- Consolidates quantitative and qualitative supplier data
- Identifies patterns across multiple contracts
- Supports fact-based supplier negotiations
- Highlights systemic issues in procurement processes

How to do it

1. Collect supplier KPIs, delivery data and feedback comments
2. Use ChatGPT to summarise common themes in qualitative feedback
3. Compute average scores and identify top and bottom performers
4. Ask AI to correlate performance issues with contract terms or conditions
5. Develop targeted improvement plans for suppliers or internal processes

Prompts

- 'Summarise recurring complaints in these supplier evaluations'
- 'Correlate late deliveries with specific manufacturing sites'
- 'Identify any biases in our rating system for suppliers'
- Chain: 'List the lowest rated suppliers by quality' → 'Suggest negotiation strategies to address their weaknesses'

Tools to use

- ChatGPT
- Power BI
- Excel

Metrics

- Reduction in late deliveries after intervention
- Improvement in supplier quality scores
- Cost savings from renegotiated contracts

Cautions

- Ensure data privacy when analysing sensitive contracts
- Avoid over-generalising qualitative comments – follow up with interviews
- Use AI insights as a starting point, not the sole basis for decisions

26. Inventory optimisation modelling using Grok

Purpose

With Grok, building straightforward inventory models becomes accessible to users without advanced data science expertise. The platform provides intuitive tools that simplify the modelling process, allowing consultants and supply chain professionals to focus on practical outcomes rather than technical details.

Grok can automatically generate key calculations essential for effective inventory management, such as Economic Order Quantity (EOQ), safety stock estimates, and reorder point analysis. By leveraging historical demand, variability, and cost data, users can obtain actionable insights tailored to their specific supply chain needs.

These capabilities empower teams to optimise inventory levels, test different scenarios, and drive data-driven decision-making. The user-friendly nature of Grok ensures that valuable analytical support is available even to those without specialist modelling skills, making inventory optimisation more efficient and collaborative.

Benefits

- Reduces inventory holding costs while maintaining service levels
- Enables what-if analysis across different demand scenarios
- Accessible for consultants without advanced modelling skills
- Supports data-driven discussions with supply chain teams

How to do it

1. Gather historical demand, lead time variability and cost data
2. Prompt Grok to calculate economic order quantity and reorder points
3. Adjust parameters (e.g., holding cost, order cost) to test

sensitivities
4. Analyse results to identify inventory reduction opportunities
5. Present recommendations with clear assumptions and caveats

Prompts

- 'Calculate EOQ given annual demand of 10,000 units, holding cost €2 per unit, order cost €100'
- 'Estimate safety stock if lead time varies between 5–10 days and demand is normally distributed'
- 'How would reducing lead time by 20% impact reorder points?'
- Chain: 'Create a basic inventory model from this data' → 'Visualise how total cost changes as order quantity changes'

Tools to use

- Grok
- Excel
- Supply chain textbooks

Metrics

- Inventory turnover before and after optimisation
- Stock-outs per quarter
- Working capital freed from reduced inventory

Cautions

- Models rely on assumptions – validate them with stakeholders
- Don't ignore practical constraints such as minimum order quantities
- Monitor service levels to ensure cost reductions don't harm customers

27. Bottleneck analysis via Qwen

Purpose

To effectively pinpoint bottlenecks in your process, start by gathering both quantitative throughput data and qualitative narrative insights from team members. Analysing these together provides a comprehensive view of where inefficiencies may exist.

Using tools such as Qwen, you can simulate process flows and highlight the steps that most frequently cause delays or slowdowns. This approach enables you to visualise problem areas and understand the impact of each stage.

By combining data analysis with process mapping, you can prioritise improvements and develop targeted solutions. Regularly reviewing these findings helps ensure ongoing optimisation and better performance overall.

Benefits

- Quickly pinpoints constraints in multi-step processes
- Supports theory of constraints discussions with clients
- Helps quantify the impact of proposed fixes
- Encourages data-driven improvement roadmaps

How to do it

1. Map the process steps with time and capacity information
2. Ask Qwen to identify the longest path or slowest step
3. Simulate throughput if the bottleneck is improved by 10%
4. Brainstorm alternative solutions (e.g., parallel processing, additional resources)
5. Monitor changes and adjust recommendations

Prompts

- 'Analyse this process and identify the bottleneck step'
- 'If we reduce processing time at step 3 by 15%, how does overall throughput change?'
- 'Recommend ways to alleviate this constraint'
- Chain: 'Describe the capacity and demand for each step' → 'Which step limits overall capacity and why?'

Tools to use

- Qwen
- Process simulation tools
- Power BI

Metrics

- Throughput increase after improvements
- Reduction in work-in-process inventory
- Lead time reduction for the end-to-end process

Cautions

- AI simulations are approximations – validate assumptions
- Consider labour and change-management implications
- Ensure improvements in one area don't create new bottlenecks elsewhere

28. Standard Operating Procedure drafting with DeepSeek

Purpose

When developing Standard Operating Procedures, it's common to work with a mix of informal notes and interview transcripts. These sources often contain valuable details but lack structure, making it difficult to produce a unified and clear document.

DeepSeek addresses this challenge by analysing and combining fragmented information. It organises content under standard headings such as purpose, scope, and procedural steps, ensuring every aspect is covered. This process helps transform scattered data into a coherent and accessible SOP.

By synthesising multiple sources, DeepSeek not only streamlines the drafting process but also preserves important insights that might otherwise be overlooked. The result is a well-structured SOP that supports consistency and clarity across teams and operations.

Benefits

- Ensures consistency across teams and locations
- Reduces time spent formatting and writing procedures
- Captures tacit knowledge that might otherwise be lost
- Improves compliance and quality assurance

How to do it

1. Collect existing notes, checklists and transcripts of operator interviews
2. Ask DeepSeek to organise the content into standard headings (purpose, scope, steps)
3. Review the draft for accuracy and completeness
4. Add visuals or screenshots where necessary
5. Publish the SOP in the client's knowledge management system

Prompts

- 'Combine these notes and interview transcripts into a standard operating procedure'
- 'Ensure the procedure includes purpose, scope, responsibilities and step-by-step actions'
- 'Highlight any gaps or inconsistencies in the draft'
- Chain: 'List the key steps operators described' → 'Rewrite these into formal instructions with safety warnings'

Tools to use

- DeepSeek
- Notion
- Google Docs

Metrics

- Time saved in creating documentation
- Compliance audit scores post implementation
- User feedback on clarity and usability of SOPs

Cautions

- Verify that AI doesn't omit critical safety or regulatory steps
- Tailor the tone and format to the client's standards
- Encourage employees to review and own the procedures

29. Productivity dashboards with Notion AI

Purpose

Live dashboards are an effective way to track critical operational metrics in real time, supporting timely decision-making and transparency across teams. By bringing together key data points, these dashboards help managers and staff stay informed about process performance and quickly identify areas requiring attention.

Notion AI enhances this approach by aggregating data from various sources into a unified dashboard view. This integration streamlines reporting and reduces the need for manual data consolidation, making it easier to monitor progress and respond to changes as they arise.

With continuous updates and automated insights from Notion AI, organisations can drive ongoing improvements, foster collaboration, and ensure that everyone has access to the information they need for daily management routines. The result is a more efficient, data-driven workplace.

Benefits

- Provides real-time insight into process performance
- Encourages data-driven daily management routines
- Facilitates collaboration by centralising information
- Reduces reliance on disparate spreadsheets

How to do it

1. Identify the key metrics to track (e.g., throughput, yield, lead time)
2. Set up Notion databases to capture and structure data
3. Use Notion AI to summarise trends and highlight anomalies
4. Design dashboards with charts, gauges and comments
5. Review regularly with the team and update as needs evolve

Prompts

- 'Create a dashboard summarising weekly production throughput and defects'
- 'Highlight any significant deviations from target values in this dataset'
- 'Generate a summary of this month's operational performance for a team meeting'
- Chain: 'Import these CSV files into a Notion database' → 'Build a dashboard that filters by date and production line'

Tools to use

- Notion AI
- Google Sheets
- Zapier

Metrics

- Frequency of dashboard usage by managers
- Number of performance issues spotted and resolved
- Reduction in time spent preparing status reports

Cautions

- Ensure data sources are kept up to date and accurate
- Avoid overwhelming users with too many metrics
- Provide training so staff understand how to interpret dashboards

30. Equipment maintenance schedule generation using ChatGPT

Purpose

To establish an effective preventive maintenance schedule, start by collecting detailed usage data and reviewing the failure history of each asset. This information provides valuable insights into how and when equipment is used, helping to predict maintenance needs.

ChatGPT can be utilised to interpret and summarise complex manufacturer guidelines, turning technical requirements into clear, actionable maintenance steps. This ensures all recommended procedures are easy to understand and follow.

By combining actual usage patterns with expert recommendations, you can create tailored maintenance schedules that improve equipment reliability and reduce unexpected downtime.

Benefits

- Extends equipment life and reduces downtime
- Aligns maintenance frequency with actual usage patterns
- Reduces reliance on paper manuals and tribal knowledge
- Supports compliance with safety regulations

How to do it

1. Collect usage hours and failure history for each asset
2. Consult manufacturer guidelines on recommended maintenance intervals
3. Use ChatGPT to synthesise guidelines into a schedule aligned with usage
4. Create a calendar or Gantt chart to plan tasks
5. Monitor adherence and adjust intervals based on observed failures

Prompts

- 'Based on 2,000 operating hours per year, what maintenance should be done for this machine?'
- 'Rewrite this technical manual into a monthly maintenance checklist'
- 'Suggest how to adjust maintenance frequency if utilisation increases by 20%'
- Chain: 'List all maintenance activities in the manual' → 'Organise them into daily, weekly, monthly and annual tasks'

Tools to use

- ChatGPT
- CMMS software
- Excel

Metrics

- Reduction in unplanned downtime
- Maintenance compliance rate
- Cost savings from preventive versus reactive repairs

Cautions

- Cross-check AI recommendations with certified maintenance engineers
- Tailor schedules to operating conditions rather than generic guidelines
- Ensure safety procedures are clearly documented

Financial Analysis & Performance Management

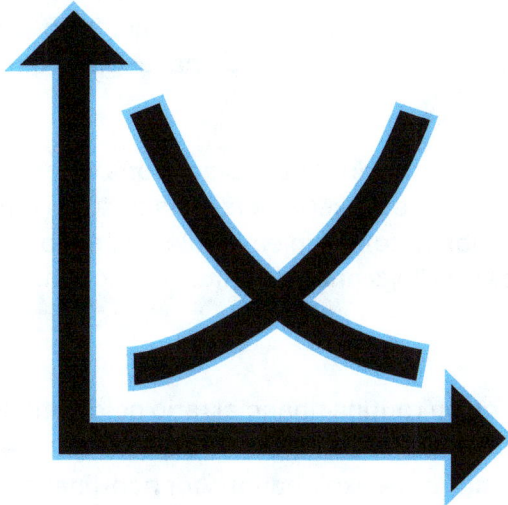

31. Financial statement analysis using ChatGPT

Purpose

Quickly interpret clients' financial statements.
Artificial intelligence streamlines the financial analysis process for consultants by automatically extracting relevant data from income statements, balance sheets, and cash flow statements. This eliminates the need for tedious manual calculations and allows professionals to focus on interpreting results.

By leveraging AI-powered tools, consultants can quickly identify important trends and anomalies across multiple reporting periods. These technologies highlight areas that require further investigation and provide clear, data-driven insights that support effective decision-making.

In addition, AI generates narrative explanations tailored for both finance and non-finance stakeholders. This ensures that complex financial information is communicated clearly, enabling all parties to understand key findings and take informed action.

Benefits

- Saves time on routine financial ratio calculations
- Identifies trends and anomalies across multiple periods
- Provides narrative explanations for non-finance stakeholders
- Supports strategic decision-making with data-driven insights

How to do it

1. Obtain recent financial statements from the client
2. Prompt ChatGPT to compute key ratios (liquidity, profitability, leverage)
3. Ask the AI to explain significant year-over-year changes
4. Benchmark results vs industry averages using external data
5. Compile a concise report highlighting strengths & weaknesses

Prompts

- 'Calculate the gross margin, operating margin and net margin from these figures'
- 'Explain why cash flow from operations declined despite higher revenue'
- 'Compare our current ratio to the industry average and assess liquidity risk'
- Chain: 'List the main components of our balance sheet' → 'Identify any red flags in asset or liability composition'

Tools to use

- ChatGPT
- Perplexity
- Excel

Metrics

- Number of actionable insights generated
- Time saved compared with manual analysis
- Accuracy of AI-computed ratios versus manual calculations

Cautions

- Validate AI calculations with accounting standards
- Beware of AI hallucinations when interpreting complex transactions
- Use AI as a supplement rather than a replacement for human judgement

32. Cash flow forecasting with Copilot and spreadsheets

Purpose

Copilot enables users to construct forward-looking cash flow models with greater speed and accuracy. By using advanced automation, it streamlines the process of building forecasting formulas directly within popular spreadsheet tools. This efficiency helps minimise manual effort and reduces the likelihood of errors occurring during model development.

In addition to automating complex calculations, Copilot facilitates scenario analysis for financial consultants and analysts. Users can quickly generate best-case, base-case, and worst-case projections by adjusting key drivers such as sales, expenses, and payment terms. This flexibility supports more informed financial planning and decision-making.

Ultimately, leveraging Copilot for cash flow forecasting improves reliability and transparency in financial models. The tool not only saves time compared to manual analysis, but also instils greater confidence in stakeholders by producing accurate and actionable insights for future business performance.

Benefits

- Speeds up model construction and reduces formula errors
- Allows consultants to explore best-case and worst-case scenarios quickly
- Facilitates better working capital management
- Enhances client confidence through more reliable projections

How to do it

1. Gather historical cash inflows and outflows
2. Use Copilot to set up forecast templates with drivers (sales, expenses, DSO/ DPO)

3. Define scenarios such as optimistic, base and pessimistic
4. Ask the AI to run sensitivity analyses on key assumptions
5. Summarise the implications of each scenario for funding needs

Prompts

- 'Build a 12-month cash flow forecast based on these historical figures'
- 'Create scenarios with 10% increase and 10% decrease in sales and show the impact'
- 'Which assumptions drive the largest changes in ending cash balance?'
- Chain: 'List all variable inputs in this model' → 'Run a what-if analysis changing each input by ±5% and summarise the results'

Tools to use

- Microsoft Copilot
- Excel or Google Sheets
- Power BI

Metrics

- Variance between forecasted and actual cash flows
- Time saved creating scenarios
- Number of funding decisions influenced by the forecast

Cautions

- Ensure underlying assumptions are realistic and agreed with stakeholders
- Remember that AI forecasts are only as good as the input data
- Communicate uncertainty clearly when presenting results

33. Cost-benefit analysis tool with Claude

Purpose

Evaluate the advantages and disadvantages associated with key strategic initiatives by conducting a thorough cost-benefit analysis. Claude provides a structured approach to this process, ensuring that both tangible and intangible factors are considered. By quantifying elements such as improved reputation, enhanced employee satisfaction, or increased stakeholder trust, Claude helps transform qualitative benefits into monetary terms. This allows for a more comprehensive understanding of the true value of an initiative.

Additionally, Claude can assist in calculating metrics like net present value and return on investment, enabling organisations to make informed decisions and prioritise projects that deliver the greatest impact.

Benefits

- Provides a consistent framework for evaluating investments
- Encourages consideration of qualitative factors alongside financials
- Helps build consensus by visualising trade-offs
- Streamlines report creation for steering committees

How to do it

1. Define the initiative and its objectives
2. List all costs (capital, operating, training) and benefits (revenue, cost savings, strategic value)
3. Use Claude to estimate qualitative benefits (e.g., improved reputation) in monetary terms
4. Calculate net present value or ROI using the AI's assistance
5. Prepare a decision matrix summarising findings

Prompts

- 'Identify all potential costs and benefits for implementing a

new CRM system'
- 'Estimate the monetary value of increased customer satisfaction'
- 'What is the payback period for this investment given these cash flows?'
- Chain: 'List intangible benefits of launching a sustainability programme' → 'Suggest methods to quantify those benefits'

Tools to use

- Claude
- Excel
- Financial calculators

Metrics

- Quality and completeness of cost and benefit items
- Stakeholder agreement on assumptions
- Percentage of projects approved or rejected based on the analysis

Cautions

- Quantifying intangibles is subjective – document assumptions clearly
- Avoid confirmation bias by considering alternative options
- Revisit analyses as new information becomes available

34. Break-even analysis generator using Perplexity

Purpose

Helping clients grasp the connection between sales volume and profitability is vital for effective decision-making. By analysing sales data, clients can identify how many units must be sold to cover fixed and variable costs, providing clarity on financial targets and risks.

Perplexity offers tools that calculate break-even points, allowing clients to assess the impact of pricing changes or cost adjustments on profitability. This insight empowers businesses to set realistic sales goals and refine their strategies for sustainable growth.

Additionally, Perplexity can summarise industry benchmarks, giving clients a broader perspective on their performance compared to competitors. Access to relevant benchmarks improves planning and helps identify areas for improvement or innovation within their market.

Benefits

- Provides a visual explanation of fixed and variable costs
- Helps determine minimum viable sales targets
- Encourages pricing discussions backed by data
- Useful for startups and new product launches

How to do it

1. Identify fixed costs (rent, salaries, overhead) and variable cost per unit
2. Use Perplexity to calculate the break-even quantity and revenue
3. Ask the AI to generate a chart showing profit at different volumes
4. Discuss how pricing or cost changes shift the break-even point
5. Incorporate findings into the client's pricing or sales strategy

Prompts

- 'Compute the break-even point given fixed costs of €100k, variable cost €5 per unit and price €12 per unit'
- 'How would a 10% price increase affect our break-even quantity?'
- 'Provide industry average contribution margins for SaaS products'
- Chain: 'List our fixed and variable costs' → 'Calculate break-even volume and illustrate it graphically'

Tools to use

- Perplexity
- Excel
- Business planning software

Metrics

- Accuracy of break-even calculations
- Client understanding of cost structures
- Impact on pricing decisions post analysis

Cautions

- Double-check cost classifications – mislabelling can distort results
- Avoid presenting break-even as a single number – highlight range of plausible outcomes
- Update assumptions as market conditions change

35. Budget variance analysis automation with Grok

Purpose

Leverage automation to streamline the monthly comparison between budgeted and actual figures. Grok can efficiently process and analyse data across all cost centres, rapidly surfacing any significant deviations from expected performance.

Once variances are detected, Grok provides insight into the underlying causes, such as price changes or volume fluctuations. By automatically pinpointing areas of concern, the tool allows teams to focus on investigating the most impactful discrepancies.

Grok suggests practical corrective actions based on the identified root causes. This enables faster course-correction within the budget cycle, supports informed decision-making, and promotes accountability by directly linking spending outcomes to responsible teams.

Benefits

- Reduces time spent on manual variance calculations
- Enables quicker course-correction within the budget cycle
- Prioritises major deviations for management attention
- Improves accountability by linking spending to responsible teams

How to do it

1. Collect budgeted and actual figures for each cost centre
2. Use Grok to compute absolute and percentage variances automatically
3. Ask the AI to flag significant variances based on thresholds
4. Investigate root causes (e.g., price changes, volume differences)
5. Prepare management commentary and recommend actions

Prompts

- 'Highlight any cost centres with more than 10% variance this month'
- 'Summarise reasons for revenue shortfalls in Q2'
- 'Suggest corrective actions for overspend on marketing'
- Chain: 'Calculate variances for each budget line item' → 'Rank them by materiality and propose follow-up questions'

Tools to use

- Grok
- Excel or Google Sheets
- Financial planning software

Metrics

- Time saved producing monthly variance reports
- Percentage of variances explained within one week
- Reduction in repeated variances in subsequent periods

Cautions

- Ensure underlying data feeds are accurate and up to date
- Don't rely solely on AI suggestions – discuss with budget owners
- Communicate variances in context, not just numbers

36. Pricing model sensitivity analysis using Qwen

Purpose

Pricing strategies play a crucial role in determining a company's overall profitability. By adjusting price points, businesses can optimise revenue, attract different customer segments, and remain competitive in the market. The impact of these changes can vary depending on volume assumptions and market responses.

Qwen enables users to rapidly test various pricing scenarios by calculating potential profits at each price level. This approach helps organisations evaluate the effects of discounts, tiered pricing, or other strategic adjustments on their bottom line.

Results generated by Qwen can be visualised using charts and heat maps, making it easier to interpret data and identify the most effective pricing strategy. These visualisations support informed decision-making and facilitate productive discussions with stakeholders.

Benefits

- Facilitates data-driven pricing decisions
- Helps identify price points that maximise profit while remaining competitive
- Enables evaluation of discount strategies and elasticity
- Supports negotiations with sales teams and clients

How to do it

1. Define the range of price points and volume assumptions
2. Use Qwen to calculate profit at each price point
3. Model the impact of discounts or tiered pricing schemes
4. Visualise results with charts and heat maps
5. Recommend pricing strategies based on sensitivity outcomes

Prompts

- 'Model profitability at price points from €10 to €20 in €1 increments'
- 'How does offering a 5% discount affect sales volume and margin?'
- 'Compare profits under a tiered pricing model versus a flat rate'
- Chain: 'List our cost per unit and fixed costs' → 'Plot profit versus price across different volume assumptions'

Tools to use

- Qwen
- Excel
- Pricing analytics software

Metrics

- Profit uplift from optimised pricing
- Win rate or conversion rate post price changes
- Customer feedback on new pricing structure

Cautions

- Ensure demand elasticity assumptions are grounded in market research
- Consider competitive reactions to price changes
- Balance short-term revenue goals with long-term brand positioning

37. Profitability by segment analysis with DeepSeek

Purpose

Profitability by segment analysis with DeepSeek helps businesses gain deeper insights into the financial performance of each customer or product segment. By examining data on revenues and associated costs, organisations can identify which segments contribute most significantly to overall profit. This approach enables more informed decision-making and strategic planning.

Understanding segment profitability allows companies to allocate resources more effectively and tailor their strategies to maximise returns. It highlights areas where pricing or operational adjustments may be beneficial. Additionally, it can uncover hidden cross-subsidisation between segments, ensuring a clearer picture of where value is created.

Regular analysis of segment profitability supports long-term growth and sustainability. It provides the foundation for decisions on investment, divestment, or strategic focus. Ultimately, leveraging DeepSeek in this process enhances both transparency and competitiveness.

Benefits

- Reveals high- and low-margin segments for targeted action
- Improves resource allocation and marketing spend
- Highlights cross-subsidisation between products or geographies
- Supports decisions to discontinue or invest in certain segments

How to do it

1. Collect revenue and cost data broken down by segment
2. Ask DeepSeek to allocate shared costs using appropriate drivers

3. Calculate contribution margin and operating profit for each segment
4. Visualise the differences with bar charts or waterfall charts
5. Discuss strategic implications with senior management

Prompts

- 'Allocate overheads to products based on labour hours and material usage'
- 'Rank customers by profitability after accounting for service costs'
- 'Identify segments with declining margins over the last 3 years'
- Chain: 'Summarise revenue and direct costs by region' → 'Calculate contribution margin and suggest actions for low-margin regions'

Tools to use

- DeepSeek
- Power BI
- Data warehouse

Metrics

- Change in profitability after implementing recommendations
- Number of products or regions restructured or discontinued
- Improvement in resource allocation efficiency

Cautions

- Allocation methods can be contentious – agree on drivers with stakeholders
- Be transparent about assumptions to avoid mistrust
- Use profitability analysis as one input among many for strategic decisions

38. KPI dashboard creation via Notion AI

Purpose

Develop interactive dashboards that track financial KPIs.
Notion AI offers the capability to collect data from a wide range of sources, enabling organisations to consolidate essential metrics into a single platform. This centralisation streamlines the monitoring process and ensures that all stakeholders have access to up-to-date information.

By leveraging Notion AI's visualisation tools, users can transform raw numbers into clear, actionable dashboards. These visual displays help teams quickly identify trends, anomalies, and progress towards key performance indicators, making data more accessible and understandable.

Incorporating these features into performance management routines enhances transparency and efficiency. Regularly updated visual dashboards empower management to make informed decisions in real time, fostering a culture of accountability and continuous improvement throughout the organisation.

Benefits

- Centralises key metrics in one accessible location
- Enhances transparency and accountability
- Reduces time spent compiling reports
- Supports real-time decision-making by management

How to do it

1. Identify the critical KPIs for the client's business (e.g., EBITDA, ROA, working capital)
2. Set up databases and templates in Notion for data entry or integration
3. Use Notion AI to summarise trends and create visualisations
4. Design a dashboard layout that highlights exceptions and targets
5. Schedule regular reviews and refine the dashboard as needs

evolve

Prompts

- 'Create a dashboard showing EBITDA, revenue growth and cash conversion cycle over the last 12 months'
- 'Highlight any KPIs that deviate from target thresholds'
- 'Generate a narrative summary of this quarter's financial performance'
- Chain: 'Import financial data into Notion' → 'Build a dashboard that compares actuals to budget and previous periods'

Tools to use

- Notion AI
- Power BI
- Spreadsheets

Metrics

- Frequency of dashboard updates and usage
- Decision turnaround time improved
- Reduction in manual report preparation effort

Cautions

- Ensure data integrity by automating data feeds where possible
- Avoid clutter – focus on a handful of KPIs tied to strategy
- Train users on how to interpret the visualisations

39. Investment appraisal support using ChatGPT

Purpose

ChatGPT can provide step-by-step guidance on investment appraisal methods such as Net Present Value (NPV), Internal Rate of Return (IRR), and payback period. By simplifying the calculations and explaining each approach, it helps consultants gain a clearer understanding of the financial implications of various projects.

Using AI, consultants can compare different investments, assess risks, and explore how changes in cash flows or discount rates impact results. This ensures more robust and informed decision-making for clients and stakeholders.

Additionally, ChatGPT can assist in drafting clear, consistent board presentations, outlining financial findings, and making recommendations based on the chosen appraisal technique. This streamlines the preparation process and enhances communication with decision-makers.

Benefits

- Simplifies complex financial calculations for non-finance stakeholders
- Provides alternative perspectives on risk and return
- Ensures consistency across different investment proposals
- Speeds up preparation of investment papers

How to do it

1. Define the investment's cash flows, discount rate and time horizon
2. Use ChatGPT to calculate NPV, IRR and payback period
3. Ask the AI to explain pros and cons of each method
4. Explore sensitivity to changes in discount rate or cash flows
5. Draft a recommendation including qualitative considerations (e.g., strategic alignment)

Prompts

- 'Compute NPV and IRR for these cash flows at a 10% discount rate'
- 'Explain why NPV is preferable to payback period in this case'
- 'How would delaying the initial investment by one year change the outcome?'
- Chain: 'Summarise the cash flows of project A and project B' → 'Recommend which project is financially more attractive and why'

Tools to use

- ChatGPT
- Financial calculators
- Excel

Metrics

- Quality of investment decision documentation
- Variance between projected and realised returns
- Stakeholder confidence in the appraisal process

Cautions

- Ensure inputs are realistic and complete before running calculations
- Explain limitations of each appraisal method to decision makers
- Consider non-financial factors (e.g., environmental impact) in recommendations

40. Financial risk scenario simulation with Copilot

Purpose

Model how external shocks (e.g.
Financial results are often influenced by a range of dynamic factors, including fluctuations in currency values and shifts in prevailing interest rates. Analysing these influences is essential for effective scenario planning within an organisation.

Copilot provides advanced support by constructing adaptable simulation models within spreadsheets, allowing users to model various scenarios with ease. These models can incorporate multiple variables and assumptions, ensuring that projections are both rigorous and responsive to market changes.

With Copilot's assistance, organisations can gain deeper insights into potential financial exposures. This enables leaders to make more informed decisions, prepare for volatility, and demonstrate robust risk management to stakeholders.

Benefits

- Prepares clients for potential market volatility
- Supports robust risk management strategies
- Encourages proactive hedging or contingency planning
- Improves board understanding of financial exposure

How to do it

1. Identify key risk drivers (exchange rates, commodity prices, interest rates)
2. Gather historical data and define plausible ranges or distributions
3. Use Copilot to build a Monte Carlo or sensitivity model in a spreadsheet
4. Run simulations to generate probability distributions of outcomes

5.   Interpret results and recommend mitigation strategies (e.g., hedging, diversification)

Prompts

- 'Create a sensitivity model showing how a ±2% change in interest rates affects our debt service cost'
- 'Build a Monte Carlo simulation with 1,000 runs for exchange rate fluctuations and report the distribution of profit outcomes'
- 'What is the probability that profits will drop below €1m under these scenarios?'
- Chain: 'List financial variables sensitive to FX movements' → 'Model how a 5% EUR depreciation impacts earnings and cash flow'

Tools to use

- Microsoft Copilot
- Excel
- Risk analysis software

Metrics

- Number of scenarios analysed and documented
- Mitigation strategies adopted by the client
- Reduction in earnings volatility over time

Cautions

- Remember that simulations are only as good as their assumptions
- Communicate uncertainty transparently and avoid a false sense of precision
- Work with finance and treasury specialists to interpret results

Digital Transformation & Technology Consulting

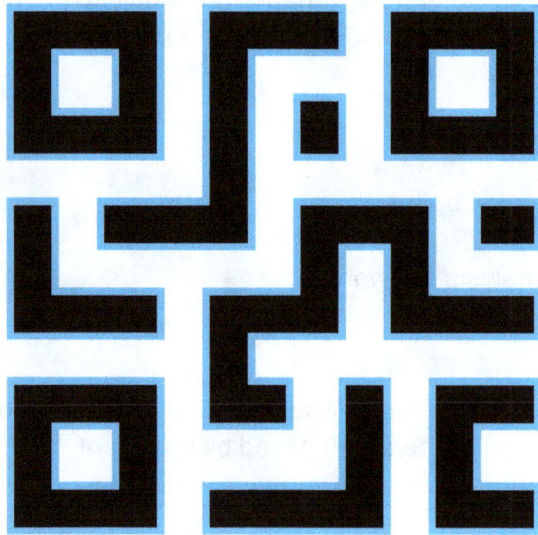

41. Digital capability assessment using ChatGPT

Purpose

Management consultants are increasingly asked to help clients understand where they stand on the digital maturity curve. This means assessing the current state of technology, processes, and skills across the business before any transformation is attempted.

ChatGPT can be a powerful partner in this phase by structuring the assessment, generating questionnaires and summarising findings. In a first conversation, the AI can help you brainstorm key dimensions of digital maturity (e.g., data governance, cloud adoption, automation, customer experience) and frame them in language that resonates with non-technical stakeholders.

In a follow-up, it can help synthesize interview notes and benchmark them against industry best practices. With its conversational tone, ChatGPT offers a fast, accessible way to organise your thoughts and prepare concise assessment reports.

Benefits

- Saves time creating digital maturity assessment frameworks and survey questions
- Helps consultants benchmark client capabilities against industry norms
- Produces clear, readable summaries for executive presentations
- Encourages a holistic view of technology, culture and processes

How to do it

1. Ask ChatGPT to outline the core dimensions of digital maturity relevant to your client's industry. The AI can highlight areas like data infrastructure, customer interfaces and organisational culture.

2.   Generate a bank of interview or survey questions for each dimension. Use prompts to tailor language to executives versus operational teams.
3.   After interviews, paste your raw notes into ChatGPT and ask it to summarise strengths, gaps and opportunities for each dimension.
4.   Request a benchmark comparison by asking ChatGPT to compare the client's maturity level with industry benchmarks (provide the benchmark data if available).
5.   Compile the AI-generated narratives into slides or reports, adding your own insights and client-specific context.

Prompts

- 'List the key dimensions that should be assessed when evaluating digital maturity in a retail company.'
- 'Draft five interview questions to understand current data governance practices for the finance department.'
- 'Summarise the following notes into strengths, weaknesses and opportunities relating to cloud adoption.'
- Chain: 'Identify common digital maturity models in manufacturing' → 'Compare our client's situation to the "digital maturity framework" and suggest where they might sit on the scale.'

Tools to use

- ChatGPT (https://chat.openai.com)
- Digital maturity model frameworks (e.g., MIT Sloan's model)
- Survey tools like Google Forms or Microsoft Forms

Metrics

- Number of stakeholders interviewed or surveyed
- Completion of a comprehensive maturity assessment covering all agreed dimensions
- Clarity and readability of the final assessment report (measured via client feedback)

Cautions

- Ensure that AI-generated questions do not bias respondents; review for neutrality and clarity
- Protect confidential data when summarising interview notes
- Digital maturity models should be adapted to the client's context rather than blindly applied

42. Digital transformation roadmap development with Copilot

Purpose

Once a client's digital capabilities are assessed, consultants must develop a clear and realistic transformation roadmap. Microsoft Copilot integrated into Excel, PowerPoint and Project can help structure this plan by breaking down initiatives into phases, estimating timelines and visualising dependencies. The purpose here is to combine your consulting expertise with AI's organisational capabilities to build a robust plan.

You might start by brainstorming transformation initiatives such as migrating legacy systems to cloud, implementing customer analytics platforms or automating back-office processes. Copilot can then translate these into a Gantt chart, assign resources and generate a high-level slide deck summarising milestones and benefits. This ensures that the plan is both comprehensive and easy to communicate to leadership.

Benefits

- Accelerates the creation of structured project timelines and milestones
- Helps visualise dependencies and resource allocation
- Provides a consistent narrative across deliverables (spreadsheets, Gantt charts, presentations)
- Supports iterative refinement as stakeholder feedback comes in

How to do it

1. Brainstorm and list all potential digital initiatives with ChatGPT. Categorise them by technology area, business unit and expected impact.
2. Use Copilot in Excel to build a table of initiatives with start dates, end dates, dependencies and assigned owners.
3. Switch to Microsoft Project or Planner with Copilot to

generate a Gantt chart, automatically calculating timelines and highlighting critical paths.

4. Ask Copilot in PowerPoint to draft slides summarising the roadmap, including timelines, KPIs and key benefits for each initiative.

5. Review the AI-generated materials to ensure feasibility, adjust timelines based on your experience and incorporate stakeholder feedback.

Prompts

- 'Create a roadmap table with columns: Initiative, Start Date, End Date, Dependencies, and Owner based on this list of digital projects.'
- 'Generate a Gantt chart showing dependencies between migrating our CRM to cloud, implementing an analytics platform and training staff on new tools.'
- 'Draft three slides summarising the digital transformation roadmap for the executive board.'
- Chain: 'List the top five risks associated with our digital transformation' → 'Suggest mitigation actions for each risk and incorporate them into the roadmap.'

Tools to use

- Microsoft Copilot in Excel, Project and PowerPoint (https://www.microsoft.com)
- Project management tools like Microsoft Project or Planner
- ChatGPT for brainstorming and risk analysis

Metrics

- Completion of a detailed roadmap covering initiatives, timelines and resources
- Alignment of the roadmap with business objectives (verified through stakeholder reviews)
- On-time sign-off of the roadmap by senior leadership

Cautions

- AI suggestions may not account for organisational politics or resource constraints; human oversight is crucial
- Adjust AI-generated timelines to reflect realistic change management pacing
- Ensure that the plan accommodates regulatory and compliance requirements

43. Cloud migration planning via Claude

Purpose

Many clients run on outdated on-premise systems that hinder scalability and agility. Planning a migration to cloud infrastructure (e.g., AWS, Azure or Google Cloud) is a complex undertaking that requires technical assessments and change management. Claude can assist by creating assessment checklists, summarising best-practice migration strategies and drafting business cases.

Consultants can use the AI to compare different cloud providers, evaluate cost models and outline a migration sequence. Claude can also help craft communications for IT and business stakeholders, explaining the rationale and benefits of moving to the cloud in clear terms. Its natural language capabilities make it useful for bridging the gap between technical details and executive summaries.

Benefits

- Saves time researching cloud migration methodologies and best practices
- Helps compare vendor offerings and build cost models
- Produces readable business cases and communications for varied audiences
- Encourages structured planning to minimise downtime and risk

How to do it

1. Provide Claude with details of the client's current IT landscape (types of applications, databases, servers) and ask for a migration readiness checklist.
2. Request a comparison of major cloud providers based on the client's needs (performance, security, compliance, cost).
3. Ask Claude to draft a high-level migration plan with phases such as assessment, pilot migration, full migration and optimisation.
4. Work with the client's IT team to validate technical assumptions and refine the plan based on real constraints.

5. Use the AI to draft an executive summary and communication plan explaining the benefits and timeline of the cloud migration.

Prompts

- 'What are the key considerations when migrating a legacy ERP system to a public cloud environment?'
- 'Compare AWS, Microsoft Azure and Google Cloud in terms of cost, scalability and compliance for a mid-sized manufacturing company.'
- 'Draft a migration plan outline with phases and key activities for moving our on-premise applications to cloud.'
- Chain: 'Identify the primary risks associated with cloud migration' → 'Suggest mitigation strategies and contingency plans for each risk.'

Tools to use

- Claude (https://claude.ai)
- Cloud provider documentation and calculators
- Cloud migration assessment tools like AWS Migration Evaluator

Metrics

- Quality of the migration readiness assessment (coverage of applications and risks)
- Cost estimates compared across cloud providers
- Stakeholder alignment on migration timeline and approach

Cautions

- Avoid sharing sensitive configuration details with AI tools
- Verify AI comparisons with official documentation and consult cloud architects
- Address data sovereignty and compliance requirements early in the planning

44. Cybersecurity risk analysis using Perplexity & Qwen

Purpose

Cyber threats are a growing concern for organisations pursuing digital transformation. Consultants need to identify vulnerabilities, understand relevant regulations and suggest mitigation strategies. Perplexity and Qwen can be used together to gather up-to-date threat intelligence, summarise cybersecurity frameworks (e.g., NIST, ISO 27001) and draft risk assessments.

Perplexity's search capabilities help pull in recent articles and reports on emerging threats, while Qwen's language understanding can summarise technical details into digestible insights for non-technical stakeholders. This pairing empowers consultants to deliver timely, authoritative cybersecurity advice without being full-time security experts.

Benefits

- Provides rapid access to current cybersecurity news and standards
- Summarises complex technical information into clear, executive-level language
- Helps identify gaps between client controls and best practices
- Supports the design of pragmatic mitigation strategies

How to do it

1. Use Perplexity to research the latest cyber threats relevant to the client's industry and summarise key takeaways.
2. Ask Qwen to explain cybersecurity frameworks like NIST or ISO 27001, focusing on controls applicable to the client's environment.
3. Create a checklist comparing the client's existing security measures with recommended controls.
4. Draft a risk assessment report highlighting critical

vulnerabilities, likelihood and potential impact.
5. Suggest mitigation actions such as security awareness training, patch management improvements or incident response planning.

Prompts

- 'What cyber threats have been reported in the financial sector in the past three months?'
- 'Summarise the key controls in ISO/IEC 27001 and how they apply to a software company.'
- 'Compare our current cybersecurity measures to the NIST Cybersecurity Framework and identify gaps.'
- Chain: 'List the top cyber risks for our client' → 'Recommend specific mitigation actions and assign responsibilities.'

Tools to use

- Perplexity (https://www.perplexity.ai) for searching recent cybersecurity news
- Qwen or ChatGPT for summarising frameworks and drafting reports
- Security benchmarking tools (e.g., CIS Controls assessment tools)

Metrics

- Number of vulnerabilities identified and categorised
- Completion of a risk assessment aligned with recognised frameworks
- Implementation of recommended mitigation measures

Cautions

- Cybersecurity is a specialised field; always involve qualified security professionals for critical assessments
- Keep client confidentiality when discussing vulnerabilities
- Ensure AI-generated recommendations comply with applicable laws and industry regulations

45. Data analytics & visualisation using Grok & Excel

Purpose

Effective digital transformation relies on data-driven insights. Consultants often need to analyse large datasets to uncover trends, correlations and performance drivers. Grok, a powerful AI tool for Python coding and data exploration, can help generate analysis scripts and recommend visualisations.

When paired with Excel, it allows consultants to quickly turn raw data into meaningful charts and dashboards. This combination enhances the consultant's ability to tell a compelling story from data, supporting evidence-based recommendations for process improvements or new product initiatives.

Benefits

- Accelerates data cleaning and analysis through AI-generated code
- Suggests appropriate visualisations tailored to the dataset and audience
- Integrates with familiar tools like Excel for easy sharing and collaboration
- Enables consultants with limited coding skills to perform advanced analytics

How to do it

1. Load your dataset into a Python environment or Excel and ask Grok to review the data structure and suggest initial exploratory analysis steps.
2. Generate Python code snippets through Grok to clean data, calculate summary statistics and run basic analyses (e.g., regression, clustering).
3. Ask Grok to propose chart types (bar, line, scatter, heatmap) that best convey the insights. Execute the code and export results to Excel if needed.

4. Use Excel's charts and pivot tables to refine the visuals and incorporate them into a dashboard or report.
5. Provide narrative context around the numbers, explaining what the trends mean for the client's business objectives.

Prompts

- 'Analyse this dataset of customer transactions and identify the top factors driving repeat purchases.'
- 'Generate Python code to clean missing values and create a correlation matrix for these variables.'
- 'Suggest visualisation types for comparing product sales across four regions over two years.'
- Chain: 'What does the regression analysis tell us about the relationship between advertising spend and revenue?' → 'Create a slide explaining the implications for our marketing budget.'

Tools to use

- Grok (https://grok.x.ai)
- Python (e.g., Pandas, Matplotlib, Seaborn libraries)
- Microsoft Excel for final visualisation and sharing

Metrics

- Number of datasets analysed and insights generated
- Quality and clarity of charts produced (assessed via client feedback)
- Actionability of the recommendations derived from data analysis

Cautions

- Data quality issues can bias the analysis; always inspect and clean the data thoroughly
- Ensure compliance with data privacy regulations when handling customer or employee data
- Don't over-interpret correlations as causation; provide appropriate caveats

46. Digital marketing strategy evaluation using Qwen

Purpose

As digital channels proliferate, clients need help evaluating the effectiveness of their marketing efforts. Qwen can synthesise marketing performance metrics (web traffic, conversion rates, social engagement) and benchmark them against industry averages. It can also suggest adjustments to targeting, channel mix or content based on the latest marketing research.

By providing a data-driven perspective on digital marketing effectiveness, Qwen empowers consultants to make actionable recommendations that drive better return on investment.

Benefits

- Aggregates diverse marketing metrics into a coherent picture
- Benchmarks performance against industry standards
- Identifies underperforming channels or campaigns
- Suggests evidence-based changes to improve marketing ROI

How to do it

1. Gather data from the client's marketing platforms (Google Analytics, social media dashboards, email campaigns).
2. Provide this data to Qwen, asking it to summarise key performance indicators and compare them to industry benchmarks (you may need to supply benchmark figures).
3. Request recommendations for reallocating budget or adjusting targeting based on the analysis.
4. Collaborate with the client's marketing team to prioritise and implement the suggested changes.
5. Monitor results over time and use Qwen to continuously refine the strategy.

Prompts

- 'Summarise our website analytics: sessions, bounce rate, conversion rate for the past quarter.'
- 'Benchmark our email campaign open and click-through rates against typical figures for the B2B software sector.'
- 'Based on this data, which marketing channels should we invest more in and which should we scale back?'
- Chain: 'Identify segments of our audience with low engagement' → 'Suggest content themes or offers that might resonate better with those segments.'

Tools to use

- Qwen (https://qwen.ai)
- Marketing analytics platforms (Google Analytics, HubSpot, Hootsuite)
- Excel or data visualisation tools

Metrics

- Improvement in key marketing metrics (conversion rate, cost per acquisition, engagement)
- Percentage of budget reallocated based on AI recommendations
- Frequency of marketing strategy reviews using AI insights

Cautions

- Benchmark data may vary by industry; ensure comparisons are appropriate
- AI recommendations should supplement, not replace, human creative judgment
- Respect privacy and data protection rules when sharing marketing data with AI tools

47. Customer journey mapping using Notion AI & Gamma

Purpose

Understanding how customers interact with a brand across touchpoints is essential for designing seamless experiences. Customer journey mapping involves visualising each step a customer takes, identifying pain points and opportunities for improvement.

Notion AI can help organise qualitative feedback and identify themes, while Gamma can transform this information into engaging visual journeys that can be easily shared with clients. These tools together make the mapping process more efficient and insightful, enabling consultants to craft customer-centric recommendations.

Benefits

- Facilitates the collection and organisation of customer feedback
- Helps visualise complex journeys in a digestible format
- Identifies pain points and opportunities across multiple touchpoints
- Enables collaborative editing and iteration with clients

How to do it

1. Gather customer feedback from surveys, interviews and support logs. Import these notes into a Notion database.
2. Use Notion AI to analyse the feedback, categorising comments by theme (e.g., onboarding experience, product usability, support response).
3. Draft a narrative for each stage of the customer journey (awareness, consideration, purchase, usage, support) based on the themes.
4. Use Gamma to create a visual journey map, placing customer actions, emotions and pain points along a timeline.

5. Present the map to stakeholders, discuss the insights and prioritise improvements.

Prompts

- 'Summarise themes from these customer interview notes, focusing on the onboarding experience.'
- 'Draft a customer journey narrative for the consideration phase based on these comments.'
- 'Generate a visual outline for a customer journey map highlighting emotions, touchpoints and pain points.'
- Chain: 'Identify the top three pain points across the journey' → 'Suggest specific interventions to address each pain point.'

Tools to use

- Notion AI (https://www.notion.so)
- Gamma (https://gamma.app) for visual narratives
- Customer feedback collection tools (SurveyMonkey, Typeform)

Metrics

- Number of journey maps created and validated with customers
- Identification of actionable improvements per journey stage
- Improvement in customer satisfaction scores after implementing recommendations

Cautions

- Journey maps rely on accurate and representative customer feedback; avoid overgeneralising from small samples
- Ensure privacy when handling and analysing customer data
- Keep journey maps updated as products, services and channels evolve

48. AI adoption planning with DeepSeek & ChatGPT

Purpose

Some clients are keen to incorporate AI into their operations but lack a structured approach for adoption. Consultants can partner with DeepSeek, a tool for exploring and prototyping AI models, and ChatGPT to identify viable use-cases, estimate benefits and design pilot programmes.

The purpose of this topic is to help consultants guide clients from ideation to implementation of AI applications such as chatbots, predictive maintenance or demand forecasting. By combining DeepSeek's technical insights with ChatGPT's conversational planning abilities, consultants can demystify AI and align pilots with business goals.

Benefits

- Helps clients identify realistic AI use-cases based on their data and processes
- Provides guidance on selecting algorithms and data requirements
- Supports creation of proof-of-concept pilots with minimal coding
- Increases confidence and buy-in for broader AI initiatives

How to do it

1. Use ChatGPT to brainstorm potential AI applications across departments (customer service, operations, sales). Gather ideas from stakeholders.
2. With DeepSeek, evaluate the data requirements and technical feasibility of each idea, including model types and training needs.
3. Prioritise use-cases based on impact and ease of implementation. Develop a pilot plan outlining objectives, timelines and success criteria.

4. Work with the client's technical team to build a prototype using low-code tools or pre-trained models available in DeepSeek.
5. Monitor pilot performance, collect feedback and decide whether to scale the AI solution.

Prompts

- 'List possible AI applications for improving supply chain efficiency in a manufacturing firm.'
- 'Evaluate the data needed to implement a predictive maintenance model for our equipment.'
- 'Draft a pilot plan for deploying a customer service chatbot including goals, timeline and success metrics.'
- Chain: 'Identify barriers to AI adoption within our organisation' → 'Develop a change management strategy to address these barriers.'

Tools to use

- DeepSeek (https://DeepSeek.ai)
- ChatGPT
- Low-code AI platforms such as Azure AI Studio or AWS SageMaker

Metrics

- Number of AI use-cases identified and evaluated
- Pilot success rates (meeting predefined goals)
- Stakeholder buy-in and readiness to scale AI solutions

Cautions

- Manage expectations; early AI pilots may not deliver immediate ROI
- Address ethical considerations such as bias, transparency and accountability
- Ensure data quality and availability before committing to AI projects

49. Technology vendor selection and RFP generation using Copilot & ChatGPT

Purpose

Selecting technology vendors (software, hardware or services) is a critical part of digital transformation. Consultants must draft requests for proposals (RFPs), evaluate vendor responses and advise on selection.

Copilot and ChatGPT can streamline this by generating RFP templates, scoring criteria and summary reports. The goal is to make vendor selection more systematic and transparent, reducing bias and ensuring alignment with client requirements. Using AI to draft and analyse documents accelerates the process and frees up consultants to focus on strategic considerations.

Benefits

- Speeds up the creation of comprehensive RFP documents
- Provides structured evaluation criteria for comparing vendor proposals
- Summarises key differences and strengths in vendor responses
- Enhances transparency and auditability of the selection process

How to do it

1. Ask ChatGPT to draft an RFP outline tailored to the specific technology category (e.g., ERP system, CRM platform). Include sections such as background, requirements, evaluation criteria and submission instructions.
2. Refine the draft based on client input and share the RFP with potential vendors.
3. When proposals arrive, use Copilot to extract key information into a comparative table (cost, features, support, compliance) and apply predefined scoring criteria.
4. Ask ChatGPT to summarise the strengths and weaknesses of

each proposal, highlighting alignment with critical requirements.

5. Facilitate a discussion with the client to select the most suitable vendor based on the analysis.

Prompts

- 'Draft an RFP for selecting a cloud-based human resources management system.'
- 'Create a scoring matrix with criteria weighted for cost, functionality, security and vendor track record.'
- 'Summarise these three vendor proposals, highlighting the best match for our requirements.'
- Chain: 'Identify potential risks in vendor A's proposal' → 'Suggest contract clauses to mitigate these risks.'

Tools to use

- ChatGPT
- Microsoft Copilot for document analysis and table creation
- Spreadsheet tools (Excel) for scoring matrices

Metrics

- Quality and completeness of the RFP document
- Time taken to evaluate vendor proposals
- Stakeholder satisfaction with the selection process

Cautions

- Ensure confidentiality of vendor proposals when using AI tools
- Verify that scoring criteria reflect the client's priorities and not generic assumptions
- Consider long-term partnerships and support beyond the proposal stage

50. Digital change management communication planning using Perplexity & Notion

Purpose

Successful digital transformation depends on effective communication and change management. Consultants must craft messages that articulate the vision, benefits and impacts of change, while addressing concerns.

Perplexity can provide research on change management best practices and stakeholder concerns, while Notion's AI can help draft tailored communications and plan training materials. The purpose of this topic is to ensure that the human side of transformation is managed thoughtfully, leveraging AI to scale communications and maintain consistency.

Benefits

- Provides evidence-based change management strategies and messaging tips
- Saves time drafting emails, announcements and training guides
- Allows collaborative editing and version control in Notion
- Helps track stakeholder concerns and responses

How to do it

1. Use Perplexity to research change management frameworks (e.g., ADKAR) and common pitfalls when introducing new technologies.
2. Identify key stakeholder groups (executives, managers, frontline employees) and list their potential concerns.
3. Ask Notion AI to draft communications tailored to each group, including announcements, FAQs and training outlines.
4. Set up a Notion workspace to track communications, feedback and training progress.

5. Monitor stakeholder sentiment and adjust messages based on feedback and adoption rates.

Prompts

- 'Summarise the ADKAR model of change management and its relevance to digital transformation.'
- 'Draft an email from the CEO announcing a new digital platform rollout.'
- 'Create a training plan for frontline staff adopting a cloud-based CRM system.'
- Chain: 'What concerns might middle managers have about automation?' → 'Draft talking points to address these concerns during a town hall meeting.'

Tools to use

- Perplexity for research
- Notion AI for drafting and collaboration
- Change management frameworks and training tools (Prosci, LinkedIn Learning)

Metrics

- Number of communication pieces drafted and delivered
- Stakeholder engagement and sentiment scores
- Adoption rates of new technologies after communications and training

Cautions

- Avoid one-size-fits-all messaging; tailor communications to different audiences
- Recognise that AI cannot replace genuine leadership involvement in change initiatives
- Monitor tone and language to ensure messages are empathetic and motivating

Risk Management & Compliance

51. Risk identification and classification using ChatGPT

Purpose

Before risks can be mitigated, they must be identified and categorised. Management consultants often begin engagements by creating a risk register that captures financial, operational, regulatory, strategic, reputational and cybersecurity risks, as described in risk consulting guides.

ChatGPT can assist by prompting comprehensive brainstorming and ensuring that less obvious risks are considered. It can also classify the risks into categories based on likelihood and impact, providing a structured starting point for analysis. By leveraging ChatGPT's knowledge of industry-specific risk factors, consultants can build a more complete picture of potential threats and design better mitigation strategies.

Benefits

- Encourages exhaustive risk identification across multiple domains
- Provides a systematic structure for the risk register
- Saves time by automating classification and preliminary assessment
- Helps uncover emerging or non-traditional risks

How to do it

1. Brief ChatGPT on the client's industry, business model and key operations. Ask it to list potential risks across financial, operational, compliance, strategic and reputational categories.
2. Review the list and prompt ChatGPT to reclassify risks by likelihood and impact (e.g., high, medium, low).
3. Create a risk register spreadsheet with columns for risk description, category, likelihood, impact and owner. Populate it using the AI-generated content and your own

insights.
4. Present the preliminary register to stakeholders for validation and add any missing risks.
5. Use the refined register as the basis for more detailed assessments and mitigation planning.

Prompts

- 'List potential operational and financial risks facing a mid-size manufacturing firm.'
- 'Categorise the following risks by likelihood and impact and suggest which ones should be prioritised.'
- 'Are there any emerging strategic or reputational risks in the hospitality industry we might overlook?'
- Chain: 'Identify compliance risks related to GDPR for our e-commerce client' → 'Suggest how these risks might be classified and prioritised.'

Tools to use

- ChatGPT
- Spreadsheet software (Excel or Google Sheets)
- Risk frameworks (ISO 31000, COSO ERM)

Metrics

- Coverage of risk categories and sub-categories
- Number of risks identified compared to industry benchmarks
- Stakeholder agreement on risk priorities

Cautions

- AI can generate generic risks; ensure each entry is relevant to the client's context
- Classification is subjective; involve cross-functional teams to validate risk ratings
- A risk register is a living document and should be updated regularly

52. Compliance checklist creation via Copilot & Notion

Purpose

Regulatory compliance is a core component of risk management. Consultants must ensure that clients adhere to applicable laws and standards (e.g., GDPR, SOX, industry-specific regulations).

Copilot and Notion can facilitate the creation of customised compliance checklists that capture regulatory requirements and map them to client processes. By automating checklist drafting and tracking, consultants can efficiently oversee compliance tasks and document evidence, reducing the risk of violations and fines.

Benefits

- Creates tailored compliance checklists quickly and accurately
- Allows collaborative tracking of compliance tasks and evidence
- Enhances transparency and accountability for regulatory adherence
- Reduces time spent on manual documentation

How to do it

1. Identify the regulatory frameworks relevant to the client's industry and operations. Compile source documents (laws, standards).
2. Ask Copilot to generate a checklist template based on the selected regulations, including each requirement, responsible party and documentation needed.
3. Import the template into Notion and customise it to reflect the client's specific processes and controls.
4. Assign responsibilities to team members, set due dates and track completion status within Notion.
5. Periodically review the checklist to ensure all compliance obligations are met and update it as regulations change.

Prompts

- 'Draft a GDPR compliance checklist for an online retailer, including data processing, consent management and breach notification requirements.'
- 'Create a SOX controls checklist for financial reporting and internal controls.'
- 'Suggest a method for tracking completion of compliance tasks across multiple departments.'
- Chain: 'Identify the key compliance obligations for a biotech company' → 'Generate a checklist with responsible roles and timelines for each obligation.'

Tools to use

- Microsoft Copilot
- Notion
- Regulatory databases and official guidance documents

Metrics

- Number of compliance requirements documented and tracked
- On-time completion rate of compliance tasks
- Reduction in compliance-related incidents or fines

Cautions

- Regulations change frequently; ensure checklists are regularly reviewed and updated
- Tailor the checklist to the client's organisational structure to avoid gaps
- Encourage a culture of compliance; checklists alone are not sufficient for good governance

53. Financial risk modelling using Claude & spreadsheets

Purpose

Beyond identifying risks, consultants often need to quantify their potential financial impact. Financial risk modelling involves stress testing and scenario analysis to estimate how changes in interest rates, currency fluctuations or market conditions could affect profitability.

Claude can help draft model structures, summarise relevant financial theory and generate scenario scripts for spreadsheets. The goal is to build robust models that inform decision-making and support the development of risk mitigation strategies.

Benefits

- Provides structured guidance on building financial risk models
- Accelerates scenario creation and analysis
- Enhances transparency by documenting assumptions and methodologies
- Supports evidence-based recommendations for risk mitigation

How to do it

1. Define the key financial variables and risk factors (e.g., revenue volatility, commodity prices, interest rates).
2. Ask Claude to suggest a modelling approach (e.g., sensitivity analysis, Monte Carlo simulation) and outline the steps in a spreadsheet.
3. Build the model in Excel or Google Sheets, incorporating formulas and data sources. Use AI to draft scenario scripts that vary the key variables.
4. Run the scenarios, analyse the distribution of outcomes and identify worst-case and best-case results.
5. Summarise the findings for management, highlighting risks

that require mitigation or hedging.

Prompts

- 'Outline a Monte Carlo simulation framework to model revenue volatility given exchange rate fluctuations.'
- 'Suggest a stress test scenario to assess the impact of a 20% decline in demand on cash flow.'
- 'Explain the difference between sensitivity analysis and scenario analysis in financial risk modelling.'
- Chain: 'Identify the financial risks associated with our supply chain' → 'Develop a spreadsheet model to quantify the impact of a supplier failure on costs.'

Tools to use

- Claude
- Microsoft Excel or Google Sheets
- Financial modelling templates or add-ins

Metrics

- Number of scenarios modelled and analysed
- Identification of critical variables driving financial risk
- Use of model outputs in risk mitigation decisions

Cautions

- Models are only as good as their assumptions; validate inputs with finance experts
- Document all assumptions and limitations for transparency
- Consider extreme scenarios that may not be captured by historical data

54. Cybersecurity vulnerability scanning & response planning using Perplexity & Qwen

Purpose

Identifying cybersecurity weaknesses and planning incident responses are vital components of risk management. Perplexity can help research common vulnerabilities, while Qwen can summarise best practices for incident response.

Together, they enable consultants to draft vulnerability assessments and response playbooks that align with recognised standards (e.g., NIST SP 800-53). This topic emphasises proactive identification and preparedness rather than reactive firefighting.

Benefits

- Provides up-to-date information on known vulnerabilities and threats
- Summarises incident response frameworks and procedures
- Helps design customised response plans for different attack scenarios
- Encourages coordination between IT, legal and communications teams

How to do it

1. Use Perplexity to find recent reports on vulnerabilities affecting the client's technology stack and summarise the key threats.
2. Ask Qwen to describe the phases of incident response (preparation, identification, containment, eradication, recovery, lessons learned) and recommend actions for each phase.
3. Create a vulnerability assessment report listing assets, identified weaknesses and remediation priorities.
4. Draft an incident response playbook detailing roles, communication protocols and decision criteria for common

attack scenarios.

5.   Conduct tabletop exercises with the client to practice and refine the plan.

Prompts

- 'List common vulnerabilities in WordPress-based websites and how they are exploited.'
- 'Summarise the NIST incident response lifecycle and key activities in each phase.'
- 'Draft an incident response plan for a ransomware attack on a manufacturing company.'
- Chain: 'Identify weaknesses in our network architecture' → 'Recommend technical and procedural controls to mitigate these weaknesses.'

Tools to use

- Perplexity for threat research
- Qwen for summarising frameworks and drafting plans
- Vulnerability assessment tools (e.g., Qualys, Nessus)

Metrics

- Number of vulnerabilities identified and remediated
- Completion of a comprehensive incident response plan
- Improvement in response times during simulations

Cautions

- Cybersecurity expertise is essential; engage specialists to validate assessments
- Do not share sensitive information (e.g., network diagrams) with AI tools
- Regularly update plans as threats evolve and technology changes

55. Supply chain risk mapping with ChatGPT & DeepSeek

Purpose

Global supply chains expose companies to a variety of risks, including supplier failures, geopolitical events and natural disasters. Consultants need to map these risks and advise on mitigation measures such as diversification or contingency planning.

ChatGPT can help identify potential risk factors across tiers of suppliers, while DeepSeek can analyse data on supplier performance, geopolitical indices and logistics. Together, they enable the creation of a comprehensive supply chain risk map that informs strategy decisions.

Benefits

- Identifies multi-tier supply chain vulnerabilities and dependencies
- Enables data-driven prioritisation of supplier risks
- Supports recommendations on diversification and contingency plans
- Enhances client preparedness for disruptions

How to do it

1. Ask ChatGPT to outline common supply chain risks (e.g., single-source suppliers, political instability, transportation bottlenecks) relevant to the client's industry.
2. Collect data on suppliers, including location, criticality, past performance and financial health. Use DeepSeek to analyse patterns and identify high-risk suppliers.
3. Create a visual risk map showing suppliers, their risk scores and potential points of failure.
4. Discuss mitigation strategies such as sourcing from multiple suppliers, increasing inventory buffers or relocating production.
5. Present the findings to the client and develop an action plan

to address the most critical risks.

Prompts

- 'List typical supply chain risks for an electronics manufacturer sourcing components from Asia.'
- 'Based on this supplier data, identify which suppliers pose the greatest risk to production continuity.'
- 'Suggest diversification strategies to reduce dependency on high-risk suppliers.'
- Chain: 'What geopolitical risks could disrupt our supply chain?' → 'Recommend contingency plans for each identified risk.'

Tools to use

- ChatGPT
- DeepSeek for data analysis and visualisation
- Supply chain management software or spreadsheets

Metrics

- Number of suppliers assessed and risk-rated
- Reduction in dependence on single-source suppliers
- Implementation of contingency measures

Cautions

- Supplier data may be incomplete or sensitive; handle it confidentially
- Risk ratings are indicative; verify with on-the-ground intelligence
- Balancing resilience and cost-efficiency may require trade-offs

56. Enterprise risk dashboard using Qwen & Notion

Purpose

Leadership teams need an at-a-glance view of the organisation's risk profile to make informed decisions. An enterprise risk dashboard consolidates key metrics such as risk exposure, mitigation status and trend indicators into a single interface.

Qwen can assist by summarising complex risk data and recommending visualisations, while Notion provides an editable workspace for collaboration. Together they empower consultants to deliver a dynamic dashboard that keeps risks visible and front of mind.

Benefits

- Provides real-time visibility into risk status and trends
- Facilitates communication and collaboration across departments
- Enables data-driven prioritisation of risk mitigation efforts
- Supports board reporting and regulatory compliance

How to do it

1. Determine the key risk metrics to be tracked (e.g., number of high-risk issues, mitigation progress, risk trend index).
2. Gather data from risk registers, audit reports and incident logs. Use Qwen to summarise the data and suggest how to visualise it (charts, heat maps, gauges).
3. Build a dashboard in Notion or a similar tool, incorporating tables, charts and narrative summaries.
4. Set up automatic data updates or regular refresh schedules to keep the dashboard current.
5. Share the dashboard with stakeholders and refine it based on feedback.

Prompts

- 'What key metrics should be included in an enterprise risk dashboard for a healthcare organisation?'
- 'Summarise trends in our risk register over the past year and suggest visualisations.'
- 'Draft an executive summary for the dashboard that highlights the most urgent risks.'
- Chain: 'Identify which risks have been open for more than six months' → 'Prioritise these risks for escalation and assign next steps.'

Tools to use

- Qwen for summarising data and suggesting visuals
- Notion or other dashboard tools (e.g., Power BI, Tableau)
- Data integration tools (Zapier, API connectors)

Metrics

- Dashboard completeness (covering all critical risk categories)
- Frequency of updates and user access
- Actions taken as a result of dashboard insights

Cautions

- Ensure data accuracy; stale or incorrect data undermines confidence
- Balance detail with clarity; dashboards should be easy to interpret
- Protect sensitive risk data by controlling access to the dashboard

57. Emerging risk monitoring using Perplexity & Qwen

Purpose

Risks evolve over time as new technologies, regulations and geopolitical events emerge. Consultants need to monitor the environment for emerging risks to help clients stay ahead.

Perplexity can scan news and research to identify relevant developments, while Qwen can synthesise insights and suggest their implications. This combination enables continuous risk monitoring, ensuring that the risk register remains current and that strategic plans incorporate emerging issues.

Benefits

- Provides early warning of emerging risks
- Saves time by filtering vast amounts of information into relevant insights
- Enhances strategic agility by anticipating potential disruptions
- Supports proactive adaptation of risk mitigation strategies

How to do it

1. Set up search queries in Perplexity for key risk-related topics (e.g., new regulations, geopolitical tensions, technological breakthroughs) and schedule regular summaries.
2. Ask Qwen to synthesise the findings and highlight implications for the client's industry and operations.
3. Update the risk register with new entries or adjust existing risks based on the insights.
4. Present a periodic emerging risk report to leadership with recommendations for monitoring or immediate action.
5. Incorporate emerging risks into scenario planning and strategic discussions.

Prompts

- 'Summarise recent regulatory developments affecting data privacy in Europe and how they might impact our operations.'
- 'Identify emerging technological risks associated with quantum computing.'
- 'What geopolitical events could disrupt our supply chain in the next 12 months?'
- Chain: 'Highlight any new risks appearing in the financial services sector' → 'Recommend how we should adjust our risk mitigation strategy in response.'

Tools to use

- Perplexity for ongoing research
- Qwen for synthesis and reporting
- News aggregation and alert tools

Metrics

- Frequency and relevance of emerging risk reports
- Number of emerging risks integrated into the risk register
- Management actions taken in response to emerging risks

Cautions

- Avoid information overload; focus on risks most relevant to the client
- Interpret emerging trends cautiously and avoid overreacting to unsubstantiated rumours
- Ensure data sources are credible and unbiased

58. Risk communication & reporting using Copilot & ChatGPT

Purpose

Clear communication of risk information to boards, audit committees and regulators is essential. Consultants often need to prepare risk reports, dashboards and presentations summarising risk status and actions.

Copilot and ChatGPT can accelerate this work by drafting narratives, designing slides and ensuring consistency across documents. They can also help tailor messages to different audiences, highlighting the most relevant risks for each. By streamlining risk communication, consultants ensure that decision-makers are informed and engaged.

Benefits

- Saves time drafting comprehensive risk reports
- Provides consistent messaging across multiple documents
- Tailors content to executive, operational and regulatory audiences
- Enhances clarity and persuasiveness of risk communications

How to do it

1. Use ChatGPT to draft the narrative sections of a risk report, summarising top risks, mitigation progress and future plans.
2. Ask Copilot in PowerPoint to generate slides that visualise risk data and highlight key messages.
3. Tailor the language and level of detail for different audiences (board vs. management vs. regulators).
4. Review the AI-generated materials to ensure accuracy, context and alignment with the client's risk appetite.
5. Deliver the final reports and presentations, soliciting feedback for continuous improvement.

Prompts

- 'Draft an executive summary of our risk status for the upcoming board meeting.'
- 'Create slides showing the top five risks, their risk scores and mitigation progress.'
- 'Rewrite this risk report section for a non-technical audience, removing jargon.'
- Chain: 'Identify which risks require immediate escalation' → 'Draft talking points for the audit committee discussion.'

Tools to use

- ChatGPT
- Microsoft Copilot for PowerPoint and Word
- Risk management software (for data inputs)

Metrics

- Timeliness and completeness of risk reports
- Clarity of messages as assessed by stakeholder feedback
- Actions taken by decision-makers based on the communications

Cautions

- Maintain confidentiality of sensitive risk information
- Avoid overstating risk severity; provide balanced and evidence-based narratives
- Ensure compliance with regulatory reporting requirements

59. Quantitative risk scoring & heat map generation using Grok & Excel

Purpose

Quantifying risks helps prioritise mitigation efforts. Consultants can use Grok to generate Python scripts or Excel formulas that calculate risk scores based on likelihood and impact, and then visualise them in heat maps.

This approach provides an objective basis for risk prioritisation and fosters transparent discussions with stakeholders about trade-offs. It supports a structured enterprise risk management process that aligns with recognised frameworks.

Benefits

- Automates risk scoring calculations and reduces manual errors
- Visualises risk distribution for easier understanding and prioritisation
- Facilitates comparison of risk across departments or projects
- Supports evidence-based decision-making

How to do it

1. Define a scoring methodology (e.g., likelihood and impact scales from 1 to 5). Agree on weighting factors with stakeholders.
2. Use Grok to generate Python code or Excel formulas to calculate composite risk scores.
3. Populate the model with data from the risk register.
4. Create a heat map in Excel or a Python visualisation library, with likelihood on one axis and impact on the other, and plot risks accordingly.
5. Discuss the heat map with stakeholders to prioritise high-risk items for immediate action.

Prompts

- 'Generate Excel formulas to compute a risk score based on likelihood and impact ratings.'
- 'Create a Python script that produces a risk heat map using Matplotlib.'
- 'Suggest how to weight financial, operational and regulatory risk categories differently in our scoring model.'
- Chain: 'Identify the top ten risks from our register' → 'Plot them on a heat map with recommended prioritisation.'

Tools to use

- Grok for code generation
- Microsoft Excel or Python libraries (Pandas, Matplotlib)
- Risk frameworks to inform scoring methodology

Metrics

- Accuracy and consistency of risk scores across reviewers
- Adoption of the heat map in risk review meetings
- Reduction in time required to prioritise risks

Cautions

- Scoring models are subjective; calibrate with cross-functional input
- Avoid false precision; risk scores are indicators, not absolutes
- Update scores regularly as risk conditions change

60. Internal control and compliance audit planning using DeepSeek & ChatGPT

Purpose

Audits of internal controls and compliance processes provide assurance that risks are being managed effectively. Consultants must plan these audits, define scope, develop test procedures and communicate findings.

DeepSeek and ChatGPT can assist by generating audit programmes tailored to the client's industry and risk profile, drafting sampling plans and summarising results. The aim is to ensure thorough coverage of controls while maintaining efficiency.

Benefits

- Accelerates the development of audit plans and test procedures
- Ensures that audits address relevant risks and controls
- Provides clear reporting of findings and recommendations
- Enhances consistency across multiple audits

How to do it

1. Identify the audit objectives and areas of focus (e.g., revenue recognition, cybersecurity controls, regulatory compliance).
2. Ask DeepSeek to suggest audit procedures and sampling methods appropriate for each area.
3. Use ChatGPT to draft the audit programme, including objectives, scope, control tests and sample sizes.
4. Conduct the audit, documenting test results and deviations.
5. Ask ChatGPT to summarise findings into a report with recommendations for remediation and improvement.

Prompts

- 'Draft an audit programme for testing controls over order processing and revenue recognition.'
- 'Suggest sampling techniques for auditing compliance with data privacy regulations.'
- 'Summarise audit findings and recommend corrective actions for controls that failed.'
- Chain: 'Identify high-risk areas in our internal controls' → 'Develop test steps to verify the effectiveness of these controls.'

Tools to use

- DeepSeek for technical audit procedures
- ChatGPT for drafting programmes and reports
- Audit management software (e.g., TeamMate, AuditBoard)

Metrics

- Coverage of high-risk areas in the audit plan
- Timeliness of audit completion and reporting
- Implementation rate of audit recommendations

Cautions

- Maintain independence and objectivity when using AI tools; validate AI-generated procedures with professional standards
- Protect sensitive data and ensure proper access controls during the audit
- Recognise that AI may not capture all nuances of complex controls; professional judgment is essential

Talent & Organisational Development

61. Employee engagement survey analysis via ChatGPT & Notion

Purpose

Understanding how employees feel about their work environment is critical to organisational success. Management consultants often administer engagement surveys to identify areas of satisfaction and concern.

ChatGPT can help by summarising open-ended responses into themes, while Notion provides a collaborative space to organise and share findings. This allows consultants to quickly surface insights such as communication issues, workload pressures or recognition gaps, and to recommend targeted interventions. According to talent consulting guidance, focusing on the entire employee life cycle - from recruitment to retention - requires a clear understanding of employee sentiment.

Benefits

- Rapidly identifies common themes across large volumes of survey responses
- Allows consultants to present clear, digestible insights to leadership
- Supports data-driven recommendations to improve engagement and retention
- Encourages transparency by sharing findings and action plans in Notion

How to do it

1. Collect quantitative and qualitative survey responses from employees. Export open-ended comments into a spreadsheet or text file.
2. Feed the text responses into ChatGPT and ask it to summarise key themes, sentiments and illustrative quotes.
3. Organise the summarised insights in a Notion database, categorising them by theme (e.g., workload, leadership,

teamwork).

4. Collaborate with HR and leadership to prioritise areas for improvement and draft action plans.
5. Communicate results to employees, highlighting both strengths and planned improvements.

Prompts

- 'Summarise the key themes from these employee engagement survey comments.'
- 'Identify positive and negative sentiment in the following responses and provide representative quotes.'
- 'What recommendations can we make to address concerns about career development opportunities?'
- Chain: 'Group these themes into broader categories' → 'Draft an executive summary highlighting the top three findings.'

Tools to use

- ChatGPT
- Notion for organising and sharing insights
- Survey platforms (Qualtrics, SurveyMonkey)

Metrics

- Percentage of employees who participated in the survey
- Number of themes identified and actioned
- Improvement in engagement scores in subsequent surveys

Cautions

- Ensure anonymity and confidentiality of employee responses
- Avoid overgeneralising from a small sample size
- Share both positive findings and areas needing improvement to maintain trust

62. Skills gap analysis & upskilling recommendations using Copilot & Qwen

Purpose

Rapid technological change requires organisations to continuously update employee skills. Consultants may be asked to identify gaps between current capabilities and future requirements and recommend training or hiring strategies.

Copilot and Qwen can streamline this process by analysing job descriptions, performance data and future skill needs, generating a comprehensive gap analysis. They can also suggest targeted courses, certifications or internal mobility options to close those gaps, ensuring the workforce remains competitive and engaged.

Benefits

- Provides a data-driven view of current versus required skills
- Recommends specific training programmes and learning resources
- Supports workforce planning and career development
- Helps prioritise upskilling investments by impact and urgency

How to do it

1. Gather data on existing employee skills, performance and training history from HR systems.
2. Identify future skill requirements based on industry trends and organisational strategy (e.g., digital skills, data analytics, agile methodologies).
3. Ask Copilot to generate a matrix comparing current skills to future needs and highlight gaps.
4. Use Qwen to suggest relevant training courses (online programmes, certifications, workshops) and alternative options such as internal rotations or mentoring.
5. Work with HR to develop an upskilling plan, including timelines, budgets and evaluation criteria.

Prompts

- 'Create a skills inventory for our sales team based on their job descriptions and performance evaluations.'
- 'Compare current data analytics skills across departments with the skills needed to implement predictive analytics.'
- 'Recommend specific courses or certifications to upskill marketing staff in digital advertising.'
- Chain: 'Identify the top skill gaps across the organisation' → 'Prioritise these gaps based on strategic impact and propose learning pathways.'

Tools to use

- Microsoft Copilot
- Qwen for learning recommendations
- Learning management systems (LinkedIn Learning, Coursera for Business)

Metrics

- Number of skills gaps identified and addressed
- Participation rates in recommended training programmes
- Improvement in performance metrics post upskilling

Cautions

- Ensure data privacy when analysing employee skill profiles
- Align upskilling recommendations with organisational strategy and budget
- Monitor learning programme effectiveness and adjust as needed

63. Onboarding programme design via Claude & DeepSeek

Purpose

Effective onboarding sets the tone for new hires and accelerates their integration into the organisation. Consultants may be asked to design onboarding programmes that provide clear role expectations, cultural immersion and necessary training.

Claude can help draft onboarding timelines, checklists and learning materials, while DeepSeek can suggest interactive content or microlearning modules. The goal is to create a structured yet engaging programme that reduces time to productivity and improves retention.

Benefits

- Provides new hires with a clear roadmap for their first 90 days
- Ensures consistency in onboarding experience across departments
- Incorporates engaging content and microlearning to enhance retention
- Reduces turnover by improving early employee experience

How to do it

1. Understand the roles and responsibilities of new hires and identify critical knowledge and skills needed early on.
2. Ask Claude to draft a 30-60-90 day onboarding plan, including activities such as orientation sessions, product training and mentorship meetings.
3. Use DeepSeek to identify or develop interactive modules (videos, quizzes, simulations) to make the content engaging.
4. Design a checklist for managers and HR to track onboarding tasks and milestones.
5. Collect feedback from new hires and continuously refine the programme based on their experience.

Prompts

- 'Create a 90-day onboarding plan for a new project manager in our consulting firm.'
- 'Draft an orientation session outline that introduces company culture, values and processes.'
- 'Suggest engaging microlearning modules for teaching our sales process to new hires.'
- Chain: 'Identify potential challenges new hires might face in their first month' → 'Develop support mechanisms to address these challenges.'

Tools to use

- Claude for planning and drafting
- DeepSeek for interactive content
- Learning management systems or employee onboarding platforms

Metrics

- Time to productivity for new hires
- New hire retention rate in the first year
- Feedback scores on the onboarding experience

Cautions

- Avoid overloading new hires with excessive information; pace the content
- Ensure the programme reflects organisational culture and values authentically
- Involve managers and peers in the onboarding process to build connections

64. Leadership development curriculum generation using Perplexity & Notion

Purpose

Developing effective leaders is a continuous organisational priority. Consultants often design leadership development curricula that combine self-assessment, coaching, workshops and experiential learning.

Perplexity can research best practices and modern leadership models, while Notion can be used to draft and organise programme content. This approach results in tailored curricula that build critical capabilities such as strategic thinking, emotional intelligence and change management.

Benefits

- Provides evidence-based leadership development content
- Organises modules, readings and activities in an accessible format
- Enables customisation to different leadership levels (senior, mid-level, emerging)
- Supports ongoing tracking of participant progress and feedback

How to do it

1. Define leadership competencies required for success in the organisation (e.g., visioning, coaching, decision-making).
2. Use Perplexity to research leadership development methodologies (e.g., 70-20-10 model, servant leadership) and identify relevant case studies.
3. Draft a curriculum outline in Notion, including modules, objectives, activities and recommended readings.
4. Incorporate self-assessment tools, peer feedback exercises and coaching sessions.
5. Pilot the programme with a small group, gather feedback and refine the curriculum before wider rollout.

Prompts

- 'Summarise current best practices in leadership development for high-growth technology companies.'
- 'Draft a module outline on leading through change, including activities and discussion questions.'
- 'Suggest case studies that illustrate ethical leadership in action.'
- Chain: 'Identify gaps in our current leadership competencies' → 'Design learning interventions to address these gaps.'

Tools to use

- Perplexity for research
- Notion for curriculum drafting and collaboration
- Leadership assessment tools (360-degree feedback, Hogan assessments)

Metrics

- Participant engagement and completion rates
- Improvement in leadership competency assessments post-programme
- Impact of leadership development on employee engagement and performance

Cautions

- Customise the curriculum to the organisation's culture and strategic goals
- Balance theory with practical application and real-world scenarios
- Provide follow-up support (coaching, peer groups) to reinforce learning

65. Diversity and inclusion analytics using Grok & Qwen

Purpose

Organisations recognise that diverse and inclusive workplaces are more innovative and resilient, yet achieving diversity goals requires accurate analysis and targeted initiatives.

Grok can assist by analysing workforce demographics and compensation data, identifying representation gaps and pay inequities. Qwen can then suggest interventions such as targeted recruitment, training programmes or policy changes.

By quantifying diversity metrics and comparing them to industry benchmarks, consultants can help clients prioritise actions that foster inclusion and compliance with equal opportunity requirements.

Benefits

- Provides a clear view of diversity and representation across the organisation
- Identifies pay gaps and potential equity issues
- Suggests targeted actions to improve diversity and inclusion
- Helps track progress against goals over time

How to do it

1. Collect demographic data (e.g., gender, race/ethnicity, age) and compensation information from HR systems, ensuring privacy safeguards.
2. Use Grok to analyse representation across job levels, departments and pay bands, looking for significant disparities.
3. Ask Qwen to benchmark the organisation's metrics against industry averages and highlight areas of concern.
4. Develop an action plan with initiatives such as inclusive recruitment strategies, mentorship programmes and policy

updates.
5. Establish a dashboard to monitor progress and communicate results to stakeholders.

Prompts

- 'Analyse our workforce demographics by job level and department and identify any under-represented groups.'
- 'Calculate gender and ethnic pay gaps across the organisation.'
- 'Benchmark our diversity metrics against industry standards and suggest actions to close gaps.'
- Chain: 'Identify barriers to advancement for under-represented employees' → 'Recommend targeted programmes to address these barriers.'

Tools to use

- Grok for data analysis and visualisation
- Qwen for benchmarking and recommendations
- HR analytics tools (Workday, SAP SuccessFactors)

Metrics

- Representation ratios by level and department
- Pay gap percentages
- Progress on diversity initiatives (e.g., hires, promotions, retention)

Cautions

- Handle demographic data sensitively and in compliance with privacy regulations
- Avoid attributing causation without qualitative insights (interviews, focus groups)
- Recognise that diversity initiatives require sustained commitment and cultural change

66. Succession planning support with ChatGPT & Notion

Purpose

Succession planning ensures organisational continuity by identifying and developing future leaders. Consultants must create frameworks to evaluate critical roles, assess potential successors and outline development plans.

ChatGPT can help structure succession planning templates and suggest evaluation criteria, while Notion provides a collaborative platform for capturing talent profiles and tracking development actions. This approach supports proactive planning rather than reactive scrambling when key leaders depart.

Benefits

- Standardises succession planning processes across the organisation
- Encourages transparent discussions about future leadership
- Supports targeted development of high-potential employees
- Mitigates risks associated with sudden departures of key personnel

How to do it

1. Identify critical roles and positions within the organisation and the competencies required for each.
2. Ask ChatGPT to create a succession planning template including fields such as potential successors, readiness level, development needs and timelines.
3. Populate the template in Notion with data from performance reviews, talent assessments and manager insights.
4. Work with leadership to review the plan, agree on successors and assign development actions.
5. Monitor progress and update the plan regularly, adjusting as organisational needs evolve.

Prompts

- 'Draft a succession planning template for executive roles in a mid-sized company.'
- 'Suggest evaluation criteria for assessing potential successors' readiness and potential.'
- 'What development activities can help prepare identified successors for broader roles?'
- Chain: 'Identify gaps in our succession pipeline' → 'Recommend strategies to build a more robust talent bench.'

Tools to use

- ChatGPT
- Notion for planning and tracking
- Talent assessment tools (9-box grid, performance/potential metrics)

Metrics

- Coverage of critical roles in the succession plan
- Readiness level of successors over time
- Internal promotion rate for leadership roles

Cautions

- Succession planning should be confidential and handled with sensitivity
- Avoid bias in identifying and developing successors; use objective criteria
- Adjust the plan as business strategy and organisational structure change

67. Organisational culture diagnostics using Perplexity & Gamma

Purpose

Culture profoundly influences employee behaviour, engagement and performance. Consultants may conduct culture diagnostics to measure alignment between stated values and actual behaviours.

Perplexity can research culture assessment frameworks and questions, while Gamma can help visualise and present diagnostic results. This combination supports a structured approach to uncovering cultural strengths and areas needing change, enabling targeted interventions that align culture with strategy.

Benefits

- Provides a structured methodology for assessing organisational culture
- Encourages honest feedback through anonymous surveys or focus groups
- Visualises cultural themes and patterns for easier interpretation
- Supports recommendations to reinforce desired behaviours and address misalignments

How to do it

1. Use Perplexity to research culture assessment models (e.g., Edgar Schein's layers of culture, Denison model) and design survey or interview questions.
2. Collect input from employees via surveys, focus groups or one-on-one interviews.
3. Summarise findings into themes such as communication style, leadership approach, innovation, risk tolerance.
4. Use Gamma to create visual representations (e.g., cultural archetype charts, spider diagrams) that highlight strengths and weaknesses.
5. Facilitate workshops with leadership to discuss the findings

and design culture change initiatives.

Prompts

- 'List key dimensions commonly used in organisational culture assessments.'
- 'Draft survey questions to evaluate our company's willingness to innovate.'
- 'Summarise themes from these focus group notes about our organisational culture.'
- Chain: 'Identify areas where stated values and observed behaviours diverge' → 'Recommend initiatives to realign behaviours with desired culture.'

Tools to use

- Perplexity for research and question development
- Gamma for visualisation
- Survey tools and facilitation materials

Metrics

- Participation rate in culture assessments
- Number of cultural themes identified and addressed
- Improvement in culture-related survey scores over time

Cautions

- Ensure anonymity to encourage honest feedback
- Recognise that culture change is a long-term effort requiring leadership commitment
- Avoid labelling or stereotyping; focus on behaviours and norms

68. Training needs assessment & content creation using DeepSeek & ChatGPT

Purpose

Determining what training employees need and creating relevant content are ongoing challenges. Consultants can use DeepSeek to analyse job roles and performance data, identifying gaps between required and actual competencies.

ChatGPT can then generate training outlines, lesson plans and microlearning content tailored to those gaps. The objective is to deliver targeted training that improves performance and aligns with organisational goals.

Benefits

- Provides evidence-based training needs analysis
- Generates tailored learning content quickly
- Enhances training relevance and engagement
- Supports continuous professional development programmes

How to do it

1. Compile job descriptions, performance evaluations and competency frameworks for the roles under review.
2. Use DeepSeek to analyse the data, highlighting areas where performance falls short of expectations.
3. Ask ChatGPT to draft training outlines and specific learning objectives addressing the identified gaps.
4. Develop or curate content (videos, articles, interactive modules) that matches the learning objectives.
5. Deliver the training and evaluate its effectiveness through assessments and on-the-job performance improvements.

Prompts

- 'Analyse performance data to identify skills that need improvement for customer service representatives.'
- 'Draft a training outline for improving negotiation skills in sales teams.'
- 'Suggest microlearning modules for teaching data privacy principles to all employees.'
- Chain: 'Identify the root causes of poor teamwork in this department' → 'Design a training programme to address these root causes.'

Tools to use

- DeepSeek for data analysis
- ChatGPT for content generation
- Learning management systems

Metrics

- Number of training needs identified and addressed
- Completion and satisfaction rates for training programmes
- Improvement in performance indicators after training

Cautions

- Training should be integrated into broader talent development strategies
- Ensure content is accurate and aligns with organisational policies and values
- Monitor training effectiveness and iterate based on feedback

69. Employee value proposition messaging with Gamma

Purpose

An employee value proposition (EVP) articulates what the organisation offers to current and potential employees in terms of culture, rewards, development and purpose. Consultants may help craft EVP messaging that resonates with target talent segments and differentiates the employer in a competitive labour market.

Gamma can transform research and messaging into engaging visual narratives, enabling clients to communicate their EVP consistently across channels.

Benefits

- Clarifies the unique benefits of working for the organisation
- Attracts and retains talent by aligning expectations with reality
- Ensures consistent messaging across recruitment marketing and internal communications
- Enhances employer brand perception

How to do it

1. Conduct research on what current employees value and what potential candidates seek in an employer. Collect input from surveys, exit interviews and market research.
2. Identify key themes such as career growth, work–life balance, culture, compensation and impact.
3. Draft EVP messaging that authentically reflects the organisation's strengths and aspirations.
4. Use Gamma to create visual assets (infographics, slide decks, videos) that tell the EVP story in a compelling way.
5. Deploy the messaging across recruitment channels, onboarding materials and internal communications, and refresh it regularly based on feedback and market changes.

Prompts

- 'Summarise what our employees most appreciate about working here based on recent engagement survey comments.'
- 'Draft an EVP statement that emphasises career development and social impact.'
- 'Create an infographic layout to visualise our EVP themes for recruitment marketing.'
- Chain: 'Identify gaps between our current EVP and what candidates in our industry value most' → 'Suggest adjustments to our EVP to improve alignment.'

Tools to use

- Gamma for visual storytelling
- Survey and research tools
- Employer branding platforms (LinkedIn Careers, Glassdoor)

Metrics

- Candidate acceptance rate and quality-of-hire metrics
- Employee retention and engagement scores
- Perception of the employer brand in surveys and external reviews

Cautions

- Ensure the EVP is authentic and achievable; over-promising can damage trust
- Tailor messaging to different talent segments (graduate hires, experienced professionals)
- Continuously update the EVP as company culture and market expectations evolve

70. HR policy review and compliance via Claude & ChatGPT

Purpose

Human resources policies must comply with local labour laws, reflect organisational values and support a positive work environment. Consultants may be tasked with reviewing and updating HR policies to ensure fairness, consistency and legal compliance.

Claude can help summarise relevant regulations and best practices, while ChatGPT can draft revised policies with clear language. This ensures that policies are comprehensive, up to date and aligned with organisational goals.

Benefits

- Ensures HR policies are legally compliant and reflect best practices
- Provides clear, accessible language for employees and managers
- Supports equitable treatment and reduces disputes
- Aligns policies with organisational culture and strategy

How to do it

1. Identify the policies requiring review (e.g., code of conduct, leave policies, remote work guidelines) and collect existing documents.
2. Use Claude to summarise relevant employment laws and industry standards applicable to the organisation's location(s).
3. Ask ChatGPT to rewrite the policies in plain language, incorporating updates and best practices.
4. Review the drafts with HR, legal counsel and employee representatives to ensure accuracy and fairness.
5. Finalise and communicate the updated policies, providing training or Q&A sessions as needed.

Prompts

- 'Summarise the key elements of Ireland's employment law regarding parental leave and include any recent changes.'
- 'Rewrite our travel and expenses policy to make it clearer and more concise.'
- 'Draft a remote work policy that balances flexibility with accountability.'
- Chain: 'Identify gaps in our current anti-discrimination policy' → 'Recommend language to strengthen it and ensure compliance.'

Tools to use

- Claude for regulatory research
- ChatGPT for policy drafting
- Collaboration platforms (Google Docs, Notion) for review

Metrics

- Number of policies reviewed and updated
- Employee understanding and compliance with the policies (measured via surveys)
- Reduction in HR-related complaints and issues

Cautions

- Consult legal experts to verify compliance and mitigate risk
- Ensure policies are inclusive and consider diverse employee needs
- Communicate changes clearly and train managers on policy implementation

Marketing & Customer Experience

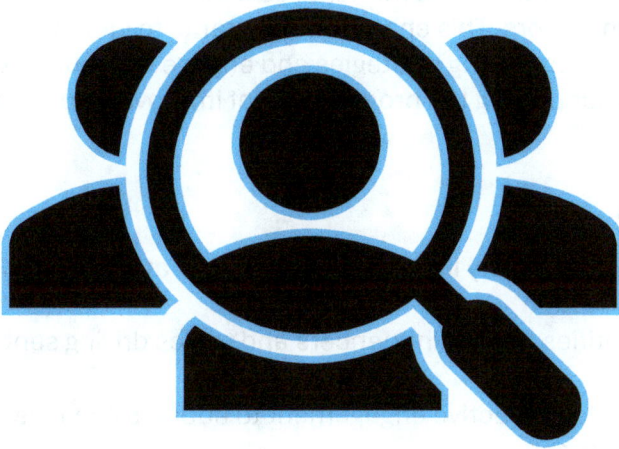

71. Social media sentiment analysis using ChatGPT & Qwen

Purpose

Understanding how customers perceive a brand in real time is essential for effective marketing and reputation management. Social media sentiment analysis involves monitoring platforms like Twitter, LinkedIn and Facebook to gauge positive, neutral and negative reactions.

ChatGPT can help summarise comments into themes and tone, while Qwen can quantify sentiment scores and benchmark them against competitors. This enables consultants to identify emerging issues, adjust marketing strategies and engage with audiences more effectively, supporting the broader goal of improving customer experience.

Benefits

- Provides timely insights into customer attitudes and brand perception
- Identifies trends, influencers and topics driving sentiment shifts
- Enables proactive engagement to address negative sentiment
- Supports data-driven marketing decisions

How to do it

1. Collect social media data using listening tools or platform APIs, focusing on brand mentions, hashtags and relevant keywords.
2. Feed the data to Qwen to perform sentiment analysis, generating scores for individual posts and overall sentiment trends.
3. Ask ChatGPT to summarise qualitative themes, highlight recurring compliments or complaints and suggest potential responses.

4. Compare sentiment metrics with those of competitors or industry benchmarks to contextualise results.
5. Present findings to the marketing team and incorporate them into campaign adjustments, customer service responses and content planning.

Prompts

- 'Analyse sentiment in these 500 tweets mentioning our brand over the last week.'
- 'Identify recurring themes in customer complaints on our Facebook page and summarise them.'
- 'Benchmark our social sentiment score against that of our main competitor.'
- Chain: 'Highlight the top positive themes driving engagement' → 'Suggest how we could reinforce these themes in upcoming campaigns.'

Tools to use

- ChatGPT for qualitative synthesis
- Qwen for sentiment scoring and benchmarking
- Social media monitoring tools (Brandwatch, Sprout Social)

Metrics

- Net sentiment score (positive minus negative) and its trend over time
- Volume of mentions across platforms
- Number of issues identified and resolved through engagement

Cautions

- Social media data may contain noise or irrelevant posts; filter carefully
- Interpret sentiment scores cautiously, considering context and sarcasm
- Ensure any engagement is coordinated with the client's communications team to avoid missteps

72. Target market segmentation & persona creation using Copilot & Notion

Purpose

Effective marketing campaigns depend on understanding distinct customer segments and crafting messages tailored to each. Consultants can use Copilot to analyse demographic, behavioural and psychographic data and Notion to organise insights into personas.

The purpose is to move beyond one-size-fits-all marketing to targeted strategies that resonate with specific groups. This aligns with the marketing consultant's role of gathering metrics and training marketing teams to reach customers more effectively.

Benefits

- Creates data-driven customer segments and detailed personas
- Improves targeting and personalisation of marketing messages
- Helps prioritise segments based on potential value
- Provides a shared understanding of customers across teams

How to do it

1. Collect customer data from CRM, website analytics and third-party sources. Variables may include age, location, purchasing behaviour, interests and values.
2. Use Copilot in Excel or Power BI to cluster customers into segments using demographic and behavioural variables.
3. For each segment, ask ChatGPT to draft a persona narrative including name, background, goals, challenges and preferred channels.
4. Organise the personas in Notion, linking data points, quotes and insights for easy reference.
5. Collaborate with the marketing team to tailor messages, offers and channels to each persona.

Prompts

- 'Segment our customer base into three groups based on purchasing frequency, product preferences and demographics.'
- 'Create a persona for a middle-aged professional who values sustainability and buys premium products.'
- 'Identify which segments are most responsive to email marketing versus social media advertising.'
- Chain: 'Describe the pain points of our budget-conscious segment' → 'Suggest marketing messages that address these pain points.'

Tools to use

- Copilot for data clustering and analysis
- ChatGPT for persona narratives
- Notion for organising personas

Metrics

- Number of actionable segments identified
- Engagement and conversion rates by segment
- ROI of campaigns tailored to each persona

Cautions

- Avoid stereotyping; base personas on data and qualitative research
- Ensure privacy compliance when handling customer data
- Personas should be revisited and updated as customer behaviour evolves

73. Customer journey analytics using Grok & dashboards

Purpose

While journey mapping focuses on qualitative experiences, journey analytics quantifies how customers move through touchpoints and where they drop off. Grok can generate scripts to track conversion funnels, time on page and cross-channel interactions, while dashboard tools (Power BI, Tableau) visualise the data.

This enables consultants to pinpoint friction points and optimise the customer experience. Integrating analytics with journey maps allows for a holistic view that combines data-driven insights with empathetic storytelling.

Benefits

- Identifies bottlenecks and drop-off points in the customer journey
- Quantifies the impact of changes to touchpoints on conversion rates
- Supports experimentation and A/B testing strategies
- Provides actionable insights for marketing, product and customer support teams

How to do it

1. Define key journey stages (awareness, consideration, purchase, post-purchase) and the metrics to track at each stage (e.g., click-through rate, time to purchase, support tickets).
2. Use Grok to generate code that extracts and analyses data from web analytics tools, CRM and support systems.
3. Build dashboards that visualise journey metrics across stages and highlight problem areas (e.g., high drop-off on checkout page, long resolution times).
4. Present the findings to stakeholders and suggest experiments (website redesign, improved onboarding,

targeted email sequences) to improve conversion and retention.
5. Monitor the impact of changes and refine the journey analytics model based on new data.

Prompts

- 'Generate Python code to calculate conversion rates between each step of our sales funnel.'
- 'Identify the pages with the highest exit rates in our online store and suggest reasons why customers abandon the process.'
- 'Create a dashboard showing customer journey metrics over the last quarter, broken down by channel.'
- Chain: 'Which journey stage has the lowest conversion rate?' → 'Propose hypotheses for the drop-off and design an A/B test to address it.'

Tools to use

- Grok for data extraction and analysis
- Dashboard tools (Power BI, Tableau, Notion)
- Web analytics platforms (Google Analytics, Adobe Analytics)

Metrics

- Conversion rate by journey stage
- Average time spent per stage
- Drop-off percentages and resolution time for support issues

Cautions

- Ensure data integration across systems is accurate to avoid misleading insights
- Consider qualitative factors (e.g., design, messaging) alongside quantitative data
- Avoid overfitting; metrics should be contextualised within broader customer behaviour trends

74. Email marketing content generation using Claude & ChatGPT

Purpose

Email campaigns remain a powerful marketing tool when they deliver personalised, relevant content. Consultants can use Claude to draft email outlines based on audience segments and ChatGPT to refine the language and tone.

This helps create campaigns that resonate with recipients, improve open and click-through rates and nurture leads through the sales funnel. By automating repetitive writing tasks, consultants can focus on strategy and testing.

Benefits

- Accelerates creation of personalised email content for multiple segments
- Ensures consistent tone and branding across campaigns
- Improves engagement metrics through tailored messaging
- Frees up time for strategic planning and analysis

How to do it

1. Identify the target segment and the objective of the email (e.g., product announcement, newsletter, limited-time offer).
2. Ask Claude to outline the email structure, including subject line ideas, key messages and call to action.
3. Use ChatGPT to write the email copy, adapting tone and style to the segment's preferences and your brand voice.
4. Personalise fields (e.g., name, previous purchase) and ensure compliance with data privacy and spam regulations.
5. A/B test different subject lines or messaging variants to optimise performance and refine the content based on results.

Prompts

- 'Draft an email announcing a new service aimed at small business owners who are price-sensitive.'
- 'Suggest subject lines that evoke curiosity without being clickbait.'
- 'Rewrite this technical update email in a friendly, accessible tone for non-technical customers.'
- Chain: 'Identify the key benefit of our product for busy professionals' → 'Write a three-paragraph email emphasising this benefit and including a call to action.'

Tools to use

- Claude for outlines and structure
- ChatGPT for language refinement
- Email marketing platforms (Mailchimp, HubSpot)

Metrics

- Open and click-through rates for each campaign
- Conversion rates (purchases, sign-ups) attributable to emails
- Unsubscribe and spam complaint rates

Cautions

- Avoid spamming; respect frequency and consent preferences
- Ensure compliance with GDPR and other data protection regulations
- Personalisation should be genuine and not creepy; use data ethically

75. Marketing performance dashboard creation via Qwen & Excel

Purpose

Marketing teams need to track campaign performance across channels and tie activities to business outcomes. Building a marketing performance dashboard allows consultants to present data on website traffic, conversion rates, cost per lead and return on investment in a single view.

Qwen can aggregate and summarise metrics, while Excel or dashboard software can visualise them. This empowers consultants and clients to make informed decisions about budget allocation, channel optimisation and campaign adjustments.

Benefits

- Consolidates marketing metrics from multiple sources into a single, coherent view
- Enables quick identification of high-performing channels and underperforming campaigns
- Supports ROI analysis and budget optimisation
- Facilitates regular performance reviews and agile adjustments

How to do it

1. Define the key metrics and KPIs that align with marketing objectives (e.g., lead generation, conversion, revenue per channel).
2. Collect data from analytics platforms, CRM and advertising dashboards (Google Ads, social media ads, email platforms).
3. Use Qwen to synthesise the data, calculate metrics such as cost per acquisition and ROI, and generate summary tables.
4. Build a dashboard in Excel, Power BI or a similar tool, displaying metrics in charts, tables and scorecards.
5. Schedule regular reviews with the marketing team to

interpret the data, celebrate successes and identify areas for improvement.

Prompts

- 'Compile our marketing metrics (traffic, conversion, cost) for each channel into a summary table.'
- 'Calculate cost per lead and ROI for our last three campaigns.'
- 'Suggest visualisations to highlight which channels deliver the highest engagement and conversions.'
- Chain: 'Identify campaigns with declining performance' → 'Recommend adjustments to improve their effectiveness.'

Tools to use

- Qwen for data aggregation and calculations
- Excel or Power BI for dashboard building
- Marketing analytics platforms (Google Analytics, HubSpot)

Metrics

- Time saved in compiling and presenting marketing data
- Conversion and ROI improvements after dashboard-driven adjustments
- Frequency of dashboard usage by stakeholders

Cautions

- Ensure data accuracy and completeness across sources; reconcile discrepancies
- Tailor dashboards to the audience (executives vs. marketing analysts)
- Avoid vanity metrics; focus on those that drive business outcomes

76. Predictive customer churn models using Perplexity & DeepSeek

Purpose

Retaining existing customers is often more cost-effective than acquiring new ones. Predictive churn models identify which customers are at risk of leaving so organisations can take proactive steps to retain them.

Perplexity can source articles and case studies on churn modelling methods, while DeepSeek can help build prototype models using client data.

Consultants can use these insights to advise clients on segmentation, retention strategies and personalised offers.

Benefits

- Enables early identification of at-risk customers
- Supports targeted retention campaigns and personalised offers
- Reduces churn rates and improves customer lifetime value
- Demonstrates the value of data-driven decision-making to clients

How to do it

1. Gather historical data on customer interactions, purchases, support tickets and contract renewals.
2. Use DeepSeek to explore modelling techniques (logistic regression, random forest, survival analysis) and generate code to build a prototype churn model.
3. Ask Perplexity to provide insights on industry-specific factors that contribute to churn and examples of successful retention strategies.
4. Evaluate the model's performance using metrics like accuracy, precision and recall, and refine it by adding features or adjusting algorithms.

5. Present the findings to the client, recommending personalised interventions for high-risk segments (discounts, loyalty programmes, proactive support).

Prompts

- 'Summarise best practices for building customer churn models in subscription-based businesses.'
- 'Generate Python code to train a churn prediction model using our customer dataset.'
- 'Identify which features (e.g., usage frequency, customer service interactions) are most predictive of churn.'
- Chain: 'Segment customers based on their churn probability' → 'Recommend specific retention actions for each segment.'

Tools to use

- Perplexity for research
- DeepSeek for modelling and code generation
- Data science libraries (Scikit-learn, TensorFlow)

Metrics

- Model accuracy and predictive power
- Reduction in churn rate after implementing recommendations
- Increase in customer lifetime value

Cautions

- Ensure data quality and completeness; missing or biased data can affect model accuracy
- Respect data privacy and ethical considerations when using customer data
- Models should be tested and validated before deployment; involve data scientists where possible

77. Customer survey design & analysis with ChatGPT & Qwen

Purpose

Surveys are a traditional yet powerful tool for gathering customer feedback on products, services and experiences. Designing effective surveys and analysing results require careful attention to question wording, response scales and statistical interpretation.

ChatGPT can help draft questions that are unbiased and easy to understand, while Qwen can analyse responses and visualise findings. This ensures that consultants deliver actionable insights from survey data, supporting improvements to products and customer experience.

Benefits

- Produces clear, unbiased survey questions tailored to research objectives
- Simplifies analysis of quantitative and qualitative data
- Highlights key findings and trends for decision-makers
- Enhances customer feedback loops and continuous improvement

How to do it

1. Define the objectives of the survey (e.g., product satisfaction, service quality, brand perception) and target audience.
2. Use ChatGPT to draft questions, ensuring neutrality and clarity. Include a mix of rating scales, multiple-choice and open-ended questions.
3. Deploy the survey through appropriate channels (email, website pop-up, social media) using a survey platform.
4. Collect responses and use Qwen to analyse quantitative data (mean scores, distributions) and summarise themes from open-ended answers.
5. Present the findings in a concise report with

recommendations for action.

Prompts

- 'Draft 10 survey questions to assess customer satisfaction with our new mobile app.'
- 'Suggest an appropriate response scale for measuring likelihood to recommend.'
- 'Summarise the key themes from open-ended responses about our customer support.'
- Chain: 'Identify the drivers of high satisfaction scores' → 'Recommend actions to reinforce these drivers.'

Tools to use

- ChatGPT for question drafting
- Qwen for analysis
- Survey platforms (SurveyMonkey, Google Forms)

Metrics

- Survey response rate and completion rate
- Net Promoter Score (NPS) and satisfaction ratings
- Number of actionable insights derived from the survey

Cautions

- Keep surveys concise to avoid respondent fatigue
- Ensure that questions are unbiased and culturally appropriate
- Protect respondent privacy and comply with data protection laws

78. SEO and content strategy planning using Perplexity & Copilot

Purpose

Search engine optimisation (SEO) drives organic traffic and builds brand authority. Consultants can use Perplexity to research keyword trends, competitor strategies and Google algorithm updates, while Copilot helps draft content calendars and outline articles that rank well.

The aim is to design a content strategy that meets user intent, adheres to SEO best practices and aligns with the client's brand voice. This is integral to marketing consultants' role in developing and executing campaigns.

Benefits

- Identifies high-value keywords and topics with strong search intent
- Helps structure content for readability, relevance and SEO performance
- Supports planning of consistent, strategic content production
- Improves organic search rankings and web traffic

How to do it

1. Use Perplexity to research keyword trends and identify topics relevant to the client's industry and target audience.
2. Evaluate competitor content to understand what is ranking well and identify gaps or opportunities.
3. Ask Copilot to draft a content calendar with topics, target keywords, publication dates and content formats (blog posts, infographics, videos).
4. For each piece, provide a brief outline and SEO guidelines, including meta tags, headings and internal links.
5. Monitor content performance (traffic, engagement, search ranking) and adjust the strategy based on results.

Prompts

- 'Identify long-tail keywords related to sustainable fashion that have moderate search volume and low competition.'
- 'Summarise our competitor's top-ranking articles on digital transformation and highlight content gaps we could fill.'
- 'Draft a three-month content calendar focusing on customer experience topics.'
- Chain: 'Outline an article on AI in supply chain management' → 'Suggest SEO best practices for optimising this article.'

Tools to use

- Perplexity for research and competitor analysis
- Copilot for content planning and outlines
- SEO tools (Ahrefs, SEMrush) for keyword data

Metrics

- Organic traffic growth and keyword ranking improvements
- Number of high-quality content pieces produced
- Engagement metrics (time on page, social shares, backlinks)

Cautions

- Avoid keyword stuffing; prioritise reader value and relevance
- SEO best practices evolve; stay updated on algorithm changes
- Ensure content aligns with brand voice and legal/compliance requirements

79. Personalisation and recommendation engine prototypes via DeepSeek & Qwen

Purpose

Delivering personalised experiences and product recommendations can significantly improve conversion and customer satisfaction. Consultants can use DeepSeek to explore machine learning models for recommendation systems and Qwen to define requirements and interpret results.

Building prototypes allows clients to test the impact of personalisation before investing in full-scale development. This topic demonstrates how AI can enhance customer experience and drive revenue growth.

Benefits

- Demonstrates the potential of personalisation to boost engagement and sales
- Provides a low-risk environment to experiment with recommendation algorithms
- Encourages data-driven decision-making for customer experience improvements
- Positions the consultant as a strategic partner in AI-driven marketing

How to do it

1. Define the objectives of the recommendation engine (e.g., increase average order value, cross-sell complementary products, personalise content).
2. Collect relevant data such as purchase history, browsing behaviour and customer profiles, ensuring privacy compliance.
3. Use DeepSeek to generate code for prototyping recommendation algorithms (collaborative filtering, content-based filtering, hybrid approaches).
4. Ask Qwen to summarise results and explain how different

algorithms perform in terms of accuracy and relevance.
5. Present the prototype outcomes to the client, discuss feasibility and next steps for scaling the recommendation engine.

Prompts

- 'Generate Python code to build a collaborative filtering recommendation engine using our product purchase data.'
- 'Compare the performance of content-based versus collaborative filtering for personalising article recommendations.'
- 'Suggest the data fields we should collect to improve our recommendation accuracy.'
- Chain: 'Identify segments of customers with similar purchase patterns' → 'Test different recommendation algorithms and report which performs best for each segment.'

Tools to use

- DeepSeek for modelling and code generation
- Qwen for results interpretation
- Data science libraries (Surprise, implicit)

Metrics

- Recommendation precision and recall metrics
- Increase in average order value or engagement rate
- Feedback from user testing or pilot programmes

Cautions

- Ensure compliance with data privacy laws when using customer data
- Start small with a pilot to validate assumptions before full deployment
- Recommendation algorithms can inadvertently reinforce biases; monitor outputs and adjust accordingly

80. Customer feedback summarisation and action planning using Notion & ChatGPT

Purpose

Customers provide feedback through various channels—support tickets, reviews, social media and surveys. Summarising this feedback and turning it into actionable improvements is an ongoing responsibility.

Notion can centralise feedback and track action items, while ChatGPT can categorise comments, identify common themes and propose next steps. This ensures that customer voices inform product and service enhancements, leading to improved satisfaction and loyalty.

Benefits

- Centralises disparate feedback in a single repository
- Simplifies identification of recurring issues and suggestions
- Helps prioritise improvements based on impact and frequency
- Demonstrates responsiveness to customer concerns

How to do it

1. Collect feedback from all available sources and import it into a Notion database, tagging entries by source and category.
2. Ask ChatGPT to analyse the feedback, grouping similar comments and highlighting the most frequent themes.
3. For each theme, ask ChatGPT to suggest potential improvements or solutions.
4. Use Notion to assign action items, set deadlines and track progress on implementing changes.
5. Communicate to customers how their feedback has been addressed through newsletters or support updates.

Prompts

- 'Categorise these customer feedback comments into themes such as usability, pricing, and support.'
- 'Summarise the top complaints and suggestions from our last 50 support tickets.'
- 'Recommend changes to our onboarding process based on these feedback themes.'
- Chain: 'Identify the most frequently mentioned feature request' → 'Draft a proposal for adding this feature to our product roadmap.'

Tools to use

- Notion for feedback management
- ChatGPT for analysis and suggestions
- Customer support platforms (Zendesk, Intercom)

Metrics

- Number of feedback items analysed and actioned
- Reduction in recurring customer complaints
- Improvement in customer satisfaction and Net Promoter Score (NPS)

Cautions

- Handle sensitive feedback confidentially and anonymise data where appropriate
- Avoid promising changes you cannot deliver; manage expectations
- Ensure feedback is representative of your entire customer base, not just vocal minorities

Mergers, Acquisitions & Change Management

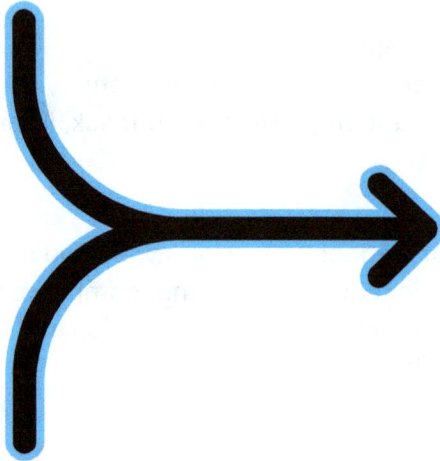

81. Due diligence document analysis using ChatGPT & Qwen

Purpose

In mergers and acquisitions (M&A), due diligence is the process of reviewing financial, legal and operational documents to identify risks and opportunities. Consultants often sift through large volumes of contracts, financial statements and regulatory filings, which can be time-consuming.

ChatGPT can summarise complex documents and highlight areas that require attention, while Qwen can cross-reference findings with industry benchmarks. This accelerates the due diligence process and ensures critical issues are identified before closing the deal.

Benefits

- Speeds up document review by summarising key points and flagging anomalies
- Enhances accuracy by comparing findings to industry standards
- Frees consultants to focus on analysis and strategic implications
- Supports comprehensive risk assessment across multiple domains

How to do it

1. Collect relevant documents (financial statements, contracts, compliance reports) from the target company, ensuring secure storage.
2. Use ChatGPT to summarise each document, extracting key terms, obligations and potential red flags (e.g., change of control clauses).
3. Ask Qwen to benchmark financial metrics against industry averages and identify any deviations that warrant deeper investigation.
4. Compile a due diligence report that consolidates the AI-

generated summaries and your own analysis of risks, opportunities and integration considerations.
5. Discuss findings with legal, financial and operational experts to validate and refine recommendations.

Prompts

- 'Summarise the key terms and obligations in this supply contract, including any clauses triggered by a change in ownership.'
- 'Analyse the target company's last three years of financial statements and identify unusual trends or outliers.'
- 'Benchmark the target's gross margin and debt levels against industry averages.'
- Chain: 'Identify potential liabilities in the target company's contracts' → 'Recommend contractual protections or indemnities to include in the purchase agreement.'

Tools to use

- ChatGPT for document summarisation
- Qwen for benchmarking and analysis
- Secure document management systems

Metrics

- Number of documents reviewed and summarised
- Issues identified and categorised (financial, legal, operational)
- Time saved compared to manual review

Cautions

- Maintain confidentiality of sensitive information and adhere to nondisclosure agreements
- AI summaries may miss subtle legal nuances; involve legal experts for final review
- Document analysis should be one component of a broader due diligence process

82. Financial synergies modelling with Copilot & Excel

Purpose

One of the key drivers of M&A value is the realisation of cost savings and revenue synergies. Consultants often develop financial models to quantify potential synergies from consolidation (e.g., reduced overheads, increased pricing power, cross-selling).

Copilot can help structure these models in Excel by creating templates that incorporate assumptions, scenarios and sensitivity analyses. The aim is to provide a realistic estimate of the combined entity's financial performance and inform negotiation and integration planning.

Benefits

- Provides a clear, structured model to quantify synergies and assess deal value
- Enables scenario analysis to test different assumptions
- Supports negotiation by illustrating potential value capture
- Assists in prioritising integration initiatives that deliver the most impact

How to do it

1. Identify potential cost and revenue synergies from the merger (e.g., shared services, procurement savings, cross-selling opportunities).
2. Ask Copilot to build a synergy model template in Excel, with inputs for assumptions, timelines and execution costs.
3. Populate the model with data from both companies and define scenarios (best case, expected case, worst case).
4. Run sensitivity analyses to understand how changes in assumptions (e.g., speed of integration, market conditions) affect synergy realisation.
5. Use the model to prioritise initiatives, support valuation discussions and track realisation post-merger.

Prompts

- 'Create an Excel model template for calculating cost savings from consolidating procurement functions.'
- 'Estimate revenue synergies from cross-selling products across the combined customer base.'
- 'Perform a sensitivity analysis on the impact of delayed integration on projected synergies.'
- Chain: 'Identify key assumptions driving synergy values' → 'Model how varying these assumptions affects the combined company's earnings.'

Tools to use

- Microsoft Copilot in Excel
- Financial modelling add-ins or templates
- M&A integration playbooks

Metrics

- Estimated value of cost and revenue synergies
- Variance between predicted and realised synergies post-deal
- Time taken to achieve targeted synergies

Cautions

- Synergy estimates are inherently uncertain; use conservative assumptions and validate with subject matter experts
- Consider integration costs and disruption when calculating net benefits
- Monitor synergy realisation closely post-merger to adjust plans as needed

83. Integration plan development using Claude & Notion

Purpose

After a deal closes, successful integration determines whether promised synergies are realised. Consultants must create detailed integration plans covering organisational structures, processes, systems and culture.

Claude can help draft integration checklists, timelines and communication plans, while Notion serves as a central hub for tracking tasks and collaboration. This ensures that activities across functions are coordinated, dependencies are managed and progress is transparent.

Benefits

- Provides a structured roadmap for integration activities
- Ensures alignment across functional teams
- Enhances visibility into progress and dependencies
- Facilitates knowledge sharing and issue resolution

How to do it

1. Identify key workstreams (e.g., finance, HR, IT, operations, culture) and appoint integration leads for each.
2. Ask Claude to create a detailed integration plan template with tasks, milestones, owners and dependencies for each workstream.
3. Build a Notion workspace to house the plan, assign tasks, set deadlines and monitor status.
4. Hold regular integration team meetings to review progress, address blockers and update the plan.
5. Communicate milestones and achievements to stakeholders to maintain momentum and transparency.

Prompts

- 'Draft an integration plan outline for merging two professional services firms, covering finance, HR, IT and operations.'
- 'Create a checklist for consolidating HR policies and systems post-merger.'
- 'Outline communication milestones for employees during the first 100 days after the merger.'
- Chain: 'Identify dependencies between IT and finance integration tasks' → 'Develop a timeline that sequences these tasks appropriately.'

Tools to use

- Claude for drafting plans
- Notion for project management
- Integration project management tools (Smartsheet, Asana)

Metrics

- Completion rate of integration tasks on schedule
- Stakeholder satisfaction with integration progress
- Realisation of planned synergies against the timeline

Cautions

- Integration plans should be flexible and adapt to emerging challenges
- Ensure that integration doesn't neglect cultural and employee experience considerations
- Over-communication is better than under-communication during integration

84. Culture integration communications via Perplexity & ChatGPT

Purpose

M&A deals often bring together organisations with distinct cultures. Failure to address cultural differences can undermine integration efforts and lead to employee disengagement.

Perplexity can research cultural integration best practices and case studies, while ChatGPT can draft communication materials that acknowledge differences and articulate a shared vision. This helps build a cohesive culture and reduces friction during the transition.

Benefits

- Raises awareness of cultural differences and similarities
- Articulates a unified vision and values for the combined organisation
- Facilitates open dialogue and addresses employee concerns
- Promotes engagement and buy-in during integration

How to do it

1. Use Perplexity to research case studies of successful and failed cultural integrations, noting best practices and pitfalls.
2. Conduct a quick culture assessment of both organisations to identify areas of alignment and divergence.
3. Ask ChatGPT to draft messaging that acknowledges cultural strengths from both sides and outlines a future cultural vision.
4. Deliver the communications through multiple channels (town halls, emails, intranet) and invite feedback.
5. Continue the dialogue with regular updates, listening sessions and actions that demonstrate commitment to the combined culture.

Prompts

- 'Summarise common challenges in integrating company cultures post-merger.'
- 'Draft a CEO message acknowledging cultural differences and committing to a shared vision.'
- 'Suggest activities to promote cultural exchange and integration among employees.'
- Chain: 'Identify cultural values common to both organisations' → 'Incorporate these values into a joint mission statement.'

Tools to use

- Perplexity for research
- ChatGPT for drafting communications
- Internal communication channels and employee engagement platforms

Metrics

- Employee understanding and alignment with the new cultural vision (measured via surveys)
- Participation in culture integration activities
- Retention rates post-merger

Cautions

- Avoid superficial messaging; demonstrate commitment through actions
- Recognise and respect cultural differences; do not force assimilation
- Keep communication two-way; listen to employee feedback and adjust plans accordingly

85. Employee attrition risk modelling with DeepSeek & Grok

Purpose

M&A announcements often trigger uncertainty among employees, leading to attrition. Consultants can use analytics to identify which employees are most at risk of leaving so targeted retention measures can be applied.

DeepSeek can help build predictive models, while Grok can generate visualisations of attrition risk across departments and demographics. This proactive approach supports talent retention and reduces disruption during integration.

Benefits

- Provides early warning of potential attrition hotspots
- Enables targeted interventions to retain critical talent
- Reduces turnover costs and knowledge loss
- Supports resource planning and leadership continuity

How to do it

1. Collect data on employee demographics, performance, engagement scores and historical attrition patterns, ensuring confidentiality.
2. Use DeepSeek to generate a predictive model that estimates the likelihood of voluntary turnover based on these variables.
3. Ask Grok to visualise attrition risk by department, tenure, role and location, highlighting areas requiring attention.
4. Work with HR to design retention strategies (e.g., stay interviews, customised development plans, retention bonuses) targeting high-risk segments.
5. Monitor attrition rates post-merger and adjust the model and strategies based on actual outcomes.

Prompts

- 'Generate Python code to build a logistic regression model predicting employee attrition based on performance and engagement data.'
- 'Visualise attrition risk by department and tenure in a heat map.'
- 'Identify the top predictors of attrition in our model and suggest actions to address them.'
- Chain: 'Flag employees with high attrition risk' → 'Draft personalised retention plans for these employees.'

Tools to use

- DeepSeek for predictive modelling
- Grok for visualisations
- HRIS systems for data

Metrics

- Model accuracy in predicting attrition
- Reduction in voluntary turnover among high-risk groups
- Cost savings from avoided replacement and disruption

Cautions

- Handle employee data sensitively and in compliance with privacy regulations
- Communicate retention initiatives transparently to avoid perceptions of favouritism
- Recognise that predictive models indicate risk but cannot predict individual behaviour with certainty

86. Synergy tracking dashboard creation using Qwen & Excel

Purpose

Achieving synergies post-merger requires ongoing monitoring to ensure that savings and revenue gains materialise. A synergy tracking dashboard provides a central view of synergy initiatives, projected versus actual savings, and status of integration activities.

Qwen can aggregate data from various workstreams, while Excel or a BI tool visualises progress. Consultants can use the dashboard to manage expectations, identify delays and adjust plans accordingly.

Benefits

- Provides real-time visibility into synergy realisation
- Facilitates accountability for integration teams
- Enables early detection of issues and quick corrective actions
- Supports communication of progress to executives and stakeholders

How to do it

1. Define synergy initiatives and metrics (e.g., headcount reduction, procurement savings, revenue synergies) and assign owners.
2. Collect baseline data and track actual savings or revenue generated after integration actions.
3. Use Qwen to summarise and aggregate data across workstreams and compute variance between projected and actual outcomes.
4. Build an Excel or Power BI dashboard that displays initiative status, financial impact and comments.
5. Review the dashboard regularly in integration meetings to celebrate wins and address gaps.

Prompts

- 'Compile data on projected vs. actual cost savings for each synergy initiative.'
- 'Highlight initiatives that are behind schedule or underperforming relative to expectations.'
- 'Suggest corrective actions for synergies that are not being realised as planned.'
- Chain: 'Identify patterns in underperforming initiatives' → 'Recommend resource adjustments or process changes to improve outcomes.'

Tools to use

- Qwen for data aggregation and analysis
- Excel, Power BI or similar dashboard tools
- Integration project trackers and ERP systems

Metrics

- Percentage of planned synergies realised
- Variance between projected and actual results
- Timeliness of completing synergy initiatives

Cautions

- Ensure data accuracy to maintain credibility
- Communicate that synergy realisation may take longer than initially forecast and adjust expectations accordingly
- Balance synergy goals with maintaining service quality and employee engagement

87. Regulatory due diligence & compliance mapping using Perplexity & Claude

Purpose

M&A transactions often involve complex regulatory considerations such as antitrust, data protection, labour laws and industry-specific regulations. Consultants must identify and map these requirements to ensure compliance and avoid deal delays or penalties.

Perplexity can research applicable regulations and precedent cases, while Claude can help draft compliance matrices and mitigation strategies. This ensures that regulatory risks are understood and managed proactively.

Benefits

- Identifies relevant regulations and potential red flags early in the process
- Assists in planning regulatory filings and approvals
- Reduces the risk of fines, litigation or deal cancellation due to non-compliance
- Provides structured documentation for regulators and stakeholders

How to do it

1. Use Perplexity to research regulatory requirements relevant to the transaction, including antitrust thresholds, industry licences and labour laws in all affected jurisdictions.
2. Ask Claude to create a compliance matrix listing each requirement, associated risks, responsible owners and timelines for action.
3. Engage legal counsel to review and refine the matrix, ensuring completeness and accuracy.
4. Incorporate regulatory considerations into the integration plan, allocating resources to address filings, notifications or remedial actions.
5. Monitor regulatory developments throughout the transaction

and adjust plans accordingly.

Prompts

- 'Summarise antitrust filing requirements for a merger of two telecommunications companies in the EU.'
- 'List data privacy regulations that could affect a cross-border acquisition involving customer data.'
- 'Draft a compliance matrix outlining regulatory requirements and responsible teams.'
- Chain: 'Identify potential regulatory hurdles in this acquisition' → 'Suggest strategies to address them in the transaction timeline.'

Tools to use

- Perplexity for regulatory research
- Claude for compliance documentation
- Legal counsel and regulatory experts

Metrics

- Number of regulatory requirements identified and addressed
- Timeliness and completeness of filings and approvals
- Incidence of regulatory issues delaying or affecting the deal

Cautions

- Regulatory landscapes vary by jurisdiction; consult local experts
- Maintain open communication with regulatory authorities to pre-empt issues
- Document all compliance efforts thoroughly to defend against potential challenges

88. Stakeholder alignment workshop facilitation using Notion & ChatGPT

Purpose

Stakeholder alignment is critical for M&A success. Workshops bring together leaders from both organisations to align on vision, objectives and roles.

ChatGPT can draft agendas, discussion prompts and facilitation guides, while Notion can capture decisions, action items and follow-up tasks. This ensures that everyone is on the same page and committed to the integration plan.

Benefits

- Provides a structured approach to aligning stakeholders on key integration issues
- Encourages open dialogue and builds trust between teams
- Captures decisions and actions for accountability and follow-through
- Helps identify potential conflicts early and resolve them collaboratively

How to do it

1. Identify key stakeholders from both organisations (executives, functional leaders, project managers).
2. Ask ChatGPT to draft a workshop agenda, including objectives, session topics (vision alignment, role clarity, success metrics) and interactive exercises.
3. Prepare materials such as presentations, discussion guides and breakout activities.
4. Facilitate the workshop, using Notion to document decisions, assigned actions and timelines in real time.
5. Follow up after the workshop to ensure actions are completed and alignment is maintained.

Prompts

- 'Create a workshop agenda to align executives on integration priorities and governance structures.'
- 'Draft discussion questions to explore potential cultural clashes and how to address them.'
- 'Suggest ice-breaker activities to build rapport among cross-company teams.'
- Chain: 'Capture key decisions made during the workshop' → 'Assign action items and owners and summarise next steps.'

Tools to use

- ChatGPT for agendas and facilitation guides
- Notion for documentation and tracking
- Virtual collaboration tools (Miro, Zoom) if remote

Metrics

- Number of alignment workshops held and attendee feedback scores
- Percentage of decisions documented and acted upon
- Reduction in miscommunication or conflict during integration

Cautions

- Ensure that all voices are heard; manage dominant personalities
- Keep workshops focused and time-bound to respect participants' schedules
- Provide clear follow-up and accountability to avoid workshop fatigue

89. Post-merger performance monitoring & analysis using Grok & Qwen

Purpose

After integration, it is essential to monitor whether the merged entity is performing as expected. Consultants can use Grok to analyse financial and operational data and Qwen to summarise trends and deviations. This continuous monitoring helps identify early warning signs of underperformance and guides corrective actions. It also provides evidence to investors and boards that the transaction is delivering promised value.

Benefits

- Tracks performance against synergy targets and financial projections
- Identifies underperforming areas for prompt intervention
- Supports transparency and accountability to stakeholders
- Encourages a data-driven approach to post-merger optimisation

How to do it

1. Define key performance indicators (KPIs) aligned with the deal rationale (revenue growth, cost savings, EBITDA margin, customer retention).
2. Gather post-merger financial and operational data from both entities' systems and integrate them into a single data warehouse.
3. Use Grok to analyse trends, variances and correlations, identifying areas where performance deviates from expectations.
4. Ask Qwen to summarise findings in executive dashboards and narrative reports, highlighting successes and areas for improvement.
5. Review the results regularly with leadership and take corrective actions where needed.

Prompts

- 'Analyse post-merger revenue trends by product line and identify variance against the integration plan.'
- 'Calculate actual cost savings achieved versus synergy projections.'
- 'Summarise operational efficiencies gained (e.g., reduced cycle times, improved service levels).'
- Chain: 'Identify areas where performance is below expectations' → 'Recommend interventions to improve outcomes.'

Tools to use

- Grok for data analysis
- Qwen for reporting and visualisation
- ERP and business intelligence systems

Metrics

- Achievement of synergy and financial targets
- Time-to-value metrics (how quickly benefits materialise)
- Number of corrective actions implemented and outcomes achieved

Cautions

- Data integration can be challenging; ensure data quality and consistency across systems
- Distinguish between integration-related issues and broader market factors when interpreting performance
- Continuous monitoring requires resources; balance depth of analysis with value generated

90. Change management training modules via DeepSeek & Gamma

Purpose

Change management is crucial for ensuring that employees adopt new systems, processes and behaviours during an M&A. Consultants can develop training modules to equip managers and employees with change management skills.

DeepSeek can generate outlines and interactive content for topics such as communication, stakeholder management and resilience, while Gamma can present the material in visually engaging slides or microlearning courses. This helps build change capability across the organisation and supports smooth transitions.

Benefits

- Builds internal change management competence
- Encourages consistent application of change management practices
- Enhances employee resilience and adaptability
- Improves the success rate of integration initiatives

How to do it

1. Identify key change management competencies needed for the integration (communication planning, stakeholder analysis, resistance management, training design).
2. Ask DeepSeek to draft a training curriculum with modules, learning objectives and recommended exercises.
3. Use Gamma to design visually appealing slides, infographics and interactive elements to support the modules.
4. Deliver the training via workshops, e-learning or blended formats, ensuring practical application through case studies and role-play.
5. Evaluate the effectiveness of the training through feedback, knowledge assessments and observation of change adoption.

Prompts

- 'Outline a training module on stakeholder analysis and engagement during organisational change.'
- 'Generate interactive exercises that teach managers how to handle resistance to change.'
- 'Design a slide deck summarising the ADKAR model and its application to our integration.'
- Chain: 'Identify common reasons for change resistance' → 'Develop a role-play scenario to practice addressing these reasons.'

Tools to use

- DeepSeek for curriculum development
- Gamma for visual design and microlearning
- Learning management systems or virtual workshop platforms

Metrics

- Participation and completion rates for training modules
- Improvement in change management competency assessments
- Employee adoption rates of new processes and systems

Cautions

- Tailor training content to the organisation's change context and culture
- Provide ongoing support and coaching beyond training sessions
- Measure the impact of training on actual change outcomes, not just knowledge retention

Sustainability & ESG

91. Materiality assessment data gathering using ChatGPT & Perplexity

Purpose

Materiality assessments identify which environmental, social and governance (ESG) issues are most important to a company and its stakeholders. Consultants must gather data from internal and external sources to determine priorities.

ChatGPT can help draft stakeholder interview questions and surveys, while Perplexity can research industry trends and stakeholder expectations. This ensures that the assessment captures the issues that have the greatest impact on business performance and stakeholder relations.

Benefits

- Ensures ESG strategies focus on topics that matter most to stakeholders and business success
- Provides a structured approach to data collection and analysis
- Saves time drafting questionnaires and synthesising research
- Aligns materiality assessments with recognised frameworks (e.g., GRI, SASB)

How to do it

1. Identify internal and external stakeholder groups (employees, customers, investors, communities, regulators) to be consulted.
2. Ask ChatGPT to draft interview guides and survey questions covering environmental, social and governance themes.
3. Use Perplexity to research ESG trends and concerns relevant to the client's industry and region.
4. Collect responses and compile secondary data from reports, news and peer benchmarks.
5. Analyse the data to prioritise ESG topics based on

stakeholder importance and business impact, and prepare a materiality matrix.

Prompts

- 'Draft survey questions to assess which ESG issues our stakeholders consider most important.'
- 'What emerging ESG trends are affecting the retail industry in Europe?'
- 'Summarise stakeholder expectations regarding climate action for a technology company.'
- Chain: 'Identify the top five material ESG issues for our company' → 'Explain why these issues are important from both stakeholder and business perspectives.'

Tools to use

- ChatGPT for drafting interviews and surveys
- Perplexity for research on ESG trends
- Survey tools and stakeholder mapping software

Metrics

- Number of stakeholders consulted and response rates
- Coverage of ESG topics in the assessment
- Stakeholder satisfaction with the materiality process

Cautions

- Ensure stakeholder diversity to avoid biased findings
- Clarify how stakeholder input will be used and communicate outcomes transparently
- Align the assessment with relevant reporting frameworks and standards

92. ESG framework comparison & selection with Copilot & Qwen

Purpose

Companies face a range of ESG reporting frameworks and standards (GRI, SASB, TCFD, CSRD, etc.), each with different focus areas and disclosure requirements. Consultants must help clients select the framework(s) that best align with their business model, stakeholder expectations and regulatory obligations.

Copilot can generate comparison tables and timelines for implementation, while Qwen can summarise framework requirements and map them to client priorities. This facilitates informed decision-making and efficient compliance.

Benefits

- Clarifies differences among ESG frameworks and standards
- Aligns reporting efforts with strategic objectives and stakeholder demands
- Simplifies the decision-making process with structured comparisons
- Provides a roadmap for phased adoption of multiple frameworks if needed

How to do it

1. Identify the frameworks and standards potentially applicable to the client (based on industry, geography and investor expectations).
2. Ask Qwen to summarise the focus areas, disclosure requirements and reporting formats of each framework.
3. Use Copilot to create a comparison table listing criteria such as relevance, complexity, stakeholder demand, regulatory mandates and implementation effort.
4. Engage stakeholders (finance, sustainability, investor relations) to evaluate the trade-offs and select the most appropriate framework(s).

5. Develop an implementation timeline, including data collection, assurance and reporting activities.

Prompts

- 'Summarise the key differences between GRI Standards and SASB Standards for a manufacturing company.'
- 'Create a table comparing TCFD climate disclosures and the EU's CSRD requirements.'
- 'Which ESG frameworks are most commonly used by companies in the technology sector, and why?'
- Chain: 'Identify the reporting standards mandated for companies operating in the EU' → 'Map these standards to our existing sustainability initiatives and data.'

Tools to use

- Copilot for comparison tables and timelines
- Qwen for summarising requirements and implications
- ESG reporting guidance documents and regulatory resources

Metrics

- Clarity of framework selection (stakeholder consensus)
- Time saved in the evaluation process
- Alignment of selected frameworks with business objectives and investor expectations

Cautions

- ESG frameworks evolve; stay informed about updates and new standards
- Avoid overburdening the organisation with multiple frameworks unless necessary
- Ensure that selected frameworks align with the organisation's material ESG issues

93. Sustainability goal dashboards via Notion & Excel

Purpose

Setting and tracking sustainability goals such as reducing carbon emissions, increasing diversity or improving community impact requires clear metrics and regular reporting. Consultants can build dashboards using Notion for narrative updates and Excel or BI tools for quantitative tracking.

This provides a transparent view of progress toward ESG targets, enabling leadership to monitor performance and take corrective action if needed.

Benefits

- Consolidates sustainability targets and progress in one accessible location
- Enables data-driven decision-making and accountability
- Demonstrates commitment to sustainability to employees, investors and regulators
- Supports continuous improvement by highlighting where targets are off-track

How to do it

1. Define specific, measurable sustainability goals aligned with material issues and frameworks (e.g., 30% reduction in scope 1 emissions by 2030, gender parity in leadership roles).
2. Collect baseline data and set up metrics for tracking progress (emissions, energy consumption, workforce demographics, community investments).
3. Use Excel or BI tools to create visual dashboards (charts, gauges, progress bars) showing actual performance against targets.
4. Maintain a Notion page that provides narrative context, explains progress, challenges and next steps.

5.   Update the dashboards regularly and review them in sustainability committees or board meetings.

Prompts

- 'Create a template to track scope 1, 2 and 3 emissions across our operations.'
- 'Design a dashboard showing diversity metrics by level, department and region.'
- 'Summarise progress against our community investment target and identify obstacles.'
- Chain: 'Identify areas where we are behind on our sustainability goals' → 'Recommend corrective actions to get back on track.'

Tools to use

- Notion for narrative and collaboration
- Excel, Power BI or Tableau for visual dashboards
- Sustainability reporting software (e.g., Enablon, Sphera)

Metrics

- Number of sustainability goals tracked and reported
- Frequency and timeliness of updates
- Progress toward targets (percentage achieved vs. planned)

Cautions

- Ensure data quality and completeness; inaccurate data undermines credibility
- Dashboards should be accessible but protect confidential information where necessary
- Consider external assurance for key sustainability metrics

94. Climate risk scenario analysis using DeepSeek & Grok

Purpose

Climate change poses physical and transitional risks to businesses, including extreme weather events, resource scarcity and regulatory shifts. Scenario analysis helps organisations understand potential impacts and develop resilience strategies. DeepSeek can generate models for climate risk scenarios based on physical and transition risk factors, while Grok can visualise results and compare scenarios. Consultants use this analysis to advise on adaptation measures and to meet regulatory requirements such as TCFD reporting.

Benefits

- Identifies potential impacts of different climate scenarios on operations and finances
- Supports strategic planning and investment decisions for resilience
- Demonstrates proactive risk management to investors and regulators
- Informs disclosures under TCFD or similar frameworks

How to do it

1. Define relevant climate scenarios (e.g., 1.5°C, 2°C, 4°C warming pathways) and time horizons (2030, 2050).
2. Use DeepSeek to model physical risks (flooding, heat stress) and transition risks (carbon pricing, policy changes) affecting the client's operations, supply chain and markets.
3. Ask Grok to visualise the financial and operational impacts under each scenario through charts, maps and stress tests.
4. Assess vulnerabilities and resilience measures, such as infrastructure upgrades, supply chain diversification or portfolio adjustments.
5. Incorporate the findings into strategic planning, disclosures and stakeholder communications.

Prompts

- 'Model the impact of a 2°C warming scenario on our logistics network, including potential disruptions from extreme weather events.'
- 'Estimate the financial effect of a carbon tax of €100 per tonne on our energy-intensive operations.'
- 'Visualise the geographic distribution of physical climate risks across our facilities.'
- Chain: 'Identify the most vulnerable parts of our value chain under the 4°C scenario' → 'Recommend adaptation measures to mitigate these vulnerabilities.'

Tools to use

- DeepSeek for scenario modelling
- Grok for visualisation and stress testing
- Climate data sources (IPCC reports, national climate risk assessments)

Metrics

- Number of scenarios modelled and analysed
- Identification of high-impact risks and mitigation measures
- Integration of climate risk insights into strategic decisions

Cautions

- Climate models involve uncertainties; provide ranges and sensitivity analyses
- Align scenarios with recognised methodologies (TCFD guidance)
- Engage climate specialists to validate assumptions and interpretation

95. Responsible supply chain evaluation via ChatGPT & Perplexity

Purpose

Sustainability extends beyond a company's own operations to its suppliers. Evaluating supplier practices related to labour conditions, environmental impact and ethical sourcing helps mitigate reputational and regulatory risks.

ChatGPT can help develop supplier questionnaires and scoring criteria, while Perplexity can research supplier performance and industry issues. Consultants use these tools to create responsible procurement strategies and encourage suppliers to improve their sustainability performance.

Benefits

- Ensures suppliers meet ethical and environmental standards
- Identifies high-risk suppliers and improvement opportunities
- Strengthens supply chain resilience and stakeholder trust
- Aligns procurement practices with ESG goals

How to do it

1. Define the sustainability criteria to evaluate suppliers (e.g., certifications, labour practices, waste management, carbon footprint).
2. Ask ChatGPT to draft supplier questionnaires and scoring models covering these criteria.
3. Use Perplexity to research suppliers' ESG performance, industry controversies and regional issues.
4. Score suppliers based on their responses and external research, and classify them into risk categories.
5. Work with procurement and suppliers to develop improvement plans, set targets and monitor progress.

Prompts

- 'Draft a supplier sustainability assessment questionnaire focusing on environmental and labour practices.'
- 'Research any ESG controversies involving our top 10 suppliers in Asia.'
- 'Develop a scoring matrix to evaluate supplier performance against our sustainability standards.'
- Chain: 'Identify suppliers with high ESG risks' → 'Recommend actions to address these risks, including supplier development or alternative sourcing.'

Tools to use

- ChatGPT for questionnaire drafting and scoring models
- Perplexity for research
- Supplier management platforms (SAP Ariba, EcoVadis)

Metrics

- Percentage of suppliers assessed for sustainability performance
- Improvement in supplier sustainability scores over time
- Reduction in incidents linked to supplier ESG issues

Cautions

- Verify information provided by suppliers; conduct audits if necessary
- Balance sustainability goals with cost and operational considerations
- Collaborate with suppliers rather than imposing unilateral requirements

96. Carbon footprint calculation & reduction planning using Qwen & Excel

Purpose

Measuring and reducing greenhouse gas emissions is central to sustainability strategies. Consultants must calculate a client's carbon footprint (scope 1, 2 and 3 emissions) and develop reduction plans. Qwen can help consolidate emissions data and perform calculations, while Excel or specialised tools track emissions over time. Consultants then use the results to set reduction targets, identify abatement opportunities and report progress.

Benefits

- Quantifies the organisation's emissions footprint across scopes 1, 2 and 3
- Identifies high-emission activities and prioritises reduction initiatives
- Supports compliance with carbon reporting requirements and net-zero commitments
- Engages stakeholders through transparent reporting and progress tracking

How to do it

1. Gather data on direct emissions (fuel use, onsite combustion), indirect emissions from purchased electricity and upstream/downstream activities (supplier emissions, business travel, product use).
2. Use Qwen to calculate emissions by applying appropriate emission factors and consolidating data into a single model.
3. Create an Excel model or use dedicated software to track emissions over time and compare against targets.
4. Identify reduction opportunities such as energy efficiency projects, renewable energy procurement, process optimisation or supplier engagement.
5. Develop a reduction roadmap with milestones and responsibilities, and integrate it into sustainability reporting.

Prompts

- 'Calculate our scope 2 emissions given our electricity consumption by region and emission factors.'
- 'Summarise the main sources of scope 3 emissions for a consumer goods company.'
- 'Identify top opportunities to reduce emissions in our transportation and logistics operations.'
- Chain: 'Develop an emissions reduction plan targeting a 50% decrease in scope 1 and 2 emissions by 2030' → 'Outline the key initiatives, investments and expected reductions for each.'

Tools to use

- Qwen for emissions calculations
- Excel or carbon accounting software (GHG Protocol tools, Sphera) for tracking
- Emission factor databases (DEFRA, EPA)

Metrics

- Total emissions measured across scopes 1, 2 and 3
- Reduction achieved relative to baseline and targets
- Cost and return on investment of reduction initiatives

Cautions

- Ensure data accuracy and completeness; emissions calculations rely on robust data
- Use recognised standards (GHG Protocol) and verified emission factors
- Consider potential trade-offs and unintended consequences of reduction measures

97. Stakeholder engagement & ESG reporting communications using ChatGPT & Gamma

Purpose

Transparent and engaging communication is essential for building trust with stakeholders on ESG matters. Consultants must craft reports, presentations and interactive content that explain the company's sustainability strategy, progress and future commitments. ChatGPT can draft narratives and highlight key messages, while Gamma can transform the content into visually compelling infographics and interactive decks. This ensures that ESG reporting is clear, engaging and aligned with stakeholders' information needs.

Benefits

- Produces clear, compelling narratives for ESG reports and presentations
- Enhances stakeholder understanding and engagement
- Supports compliance with reporting standards while telling a coherent story
- Differentiates the company's sustainability messaging through design and storytelling

How to do it

1. Gather data and stories from sustainability initiatives, including achievements, challenges and future plans.
2. Use ChatGPT to draft narratives for the ESG report, focusing on material topics and performance against goals.
3. Ask Gamma to create visual assets such as infographics, charts and slide decks that complement the narrative.
4. Tailor communications for different audiences (investors, employees, customers, regulators) with appropriate language and detail.
5. Publish the report and deliver presentations, gathering feedback for continuous improvement.

Prompts

- 'Draft an executive summary of our ESG performance over the past year, highlighting major achievements and areas for improvement.'
- 'Create an infographic explaining our carbon reduction strategy and progress.'
- 'Rewrite our sustainability messaging for a consumer audience, using plain language and storytelling.'
- Chain: 'Identify the most compelling stories from our community impact programmes' → 'Design a slide that showcases these stories visually.'

Tools to use

- ChatGPT for narrative drafting
- Gamma for visual design and interactive presentations
- ESG reporting frameworks (GRI, SASB) for structure

Metrics

- Stakeholder feedback on report clarity and engagement
- Number of views, downloads or shares of ESG communications
- Improvement in ESG ratings or investor perceptions

Cautions

- Avoid greenwashing; ensure that communications are honest and supported by data
- Tailor messaging to stakeholder needs; investors may require more detail than consumers
- Align with reporting standards to ensure completeness and comparability

98. ESG compliance checklists via Claude & Notion

Purpose

Compliance with ESG regulations and reporting standards is becoming mandatory in many jurisdictions. Consultants must ensure that clients meet these requirements by creating comprehensive compliance checklists.

Claude can summarise regulatory obligations and reporting criteria, while Notion can serve as a repository for tracking compliance tasks and documentation. This ensures that ESG reporting is accurate, timely and aligned with legal requirements.

Benefits

- Provides a structured approach to ESG compliance
- Reduces the risk of non-compliance penalties or reputational damage
- Facilitates collaboration across departments responsible for data collection and reporting
- Supports readiness for external assurance and audits

How to do it

1. Identify applicable ESG regulations and reporting standards based on the client's industry and jurisdictions (e.g., EU CSRD, SFDR, SEC climate disclosures).
2. Use Claude to summarise the specific disclosure requirements, deadlines and data needed for each standard.
3. Create a Notion checklist template listing each requirement, responsible owner, due date and documentation status.
4. Assign tasks to relevant teams (finance, HR, operations) and track progress in Notion.
5. Review the checklist regularly to ensure timely completion, update it when regulations change and prepare for external assurance.

Prompts

- 'Summarise the disclosure requirements under the EU Corporate Sustainability Reporting Directive (CSRD) for a manufacturing company.'
- 'Draft a compliance checklist for the SEC's climate disclosure rules for publicly listed firms.'
- 'Identify cross-departmental data required for ESG reporting and assign responsible owners.'
- Chain: 'Determine which ESG metrics require external assurance' → 'Plan the timeline and documentation needed for assurance.'

Tools to use

- Claude for regulatory summaries
- Notion for checklist management
- Legal and compliance resources

Metrics

- Completion rate of checklist items by deadline
- Number of non-compliance issues identified and resolved
- Readiness for external assurance as assessed by auditors

Cautions

- ESG regulations are evolving quickly; update checklists regularly
- Ensure that responsibility assignments are clear and supported by leadership
- Consider integrating checklists with broader risk and compliance management processes

99. Social impact investment evaluation with Perplexity & DeepSeek

Purpose

Investing in projects that deliver social impact alongside financial returns is a growing priority for many organisations and investors. Consultants may be asked to evaluate opportunities such as affordable housing, healthcare access or education initiatives. Perplexity can provide research on impact investment trends and case studies, while DeepSeek can model financial returns and social outcomes. This helps clients make informed decisions that align with their values and ESG objectives.

Benefits

- Identifies impact investment opportunities aligned with client goals
- Quantifies both financial and social returns
- Supports diversification of investment portfolios with ESG-aligned assets
- Enhances reputation and stakeholder trust through meaningful impact

How to do it

1. Clarify the client's social impact priorities (e.g., poverty alleviation, health, education, climate resilience) and financial return expectations.
2. Use Perplexity to research impact investment opportunities, funds and case studies relevant to the priorities.
3. Ask DeepSeek to model potential financial returns and estimate social outcomes using frameworks such as theory of change or impact metrics (e.g., number of beneficiaries, carbon avoided).
4. Evaluate the opportunities based on risk-adjusted returns, impact potential and alignment with the client's strategy.
5. Develop recommendations for investment allocation, monitoring and reporting on impact.

Prompts

- 'Identify social impact investment funds focused on renewable energy in developing countries.'
- 'Model the financial and social returns of investing €5 million in affordable housing projects.'
- 'Compare potential investments in education versus healthcare based on social outcomes and risk profiles.'
- Chain: 'Shortlist impact investment opportunities aligned with our priorities' → 'Analyse their expected returns and impact metrics to recommend a balanced portfolio.'

Tools to use

- Perplexity for research on impact investments
- DeepSeek for financial and impact modelling
- Impact measurement frameworks (GIIN's IRIS+ metrics, SDG alignment)

Metrics

- Expected and realised financial return on impact investments
- Social outcomes achieved (beneficiaries served, emissions reduced, etc.)
- Alignment of investments with client's ESG strategy and impact goals

Cautions

- Impact measurement is complex and subject to differing methodologies; choose a consistent framework
- Balance social impact with financial sustainability; avoid overemphasis on one at the expense of the other
- Ensure due diligence on impact funds and projects to mitigate risk of "impact washing"

100. Sustainability training & awareness programmes using Notion & ChatGPT

Purpose

Embedding sustainability into organisational culture requires ongoing education and engagement. Consultants can design training programmes and awareness campaigns that build understanding of ESG issues, company policies and individual responsibilities. ChatGPT can help draft training materials and interactive content, while Notion can host resources and track participation. This fosters a culture where employees feel empowered to contribute to sustainability goals and act as ambassadors for the company's ESG commitments.

Benefits

- Increases employee awareness and knowledge of sustainability and ESG topics
- Encourages behavioural changes that support company sustainability goals
- Provides a central resource hub for training materials and updates
- Improves engagement and pride in the organisation's sustainability efforts

How to do it

1. Assess the current level of sustainability awareness among employees through surveys or interviews.
2. Use ChatGPT to draft training content, including presentations, articles, quizzes and interactive scenarios that cover key ESG topics (e.g., waste reduction, energy conservation, diversity and inclusion).
3. Organise the materials in Notion, creating modules that employees can navigate at their own pace. Include discussion forums or comment sections for peer learning.
4. Launch the training programme with a kickoff event or internal marketing campaign to generate interest.

5. Track participation and knowledge retention through quizzes or follow-up surveys and use feedback to refine the programme.

Prompts

- 'Draft a training module introducing the UN Sustainable Development Goals and how our company contributes to them.'
- 'Create a quiz to test employees' knowledge of our recycling and waste management policies.'
- 'Suggest interactive activities to help staff understand implicit bias and inclusion.'
- Chain: 'Identify misconceptions employees have about sustainability based on survey responses' → 'Develop targeted content to address these misconceptions.'

Tools to use

- ChatGPT for content creation
- Notion for hosting and tracking training programmes
- Learning management systems if available

Metrics

- Participation rates in sustainability training programmes
- Improvement in sustainability knowledge scores pre- and post-training
- Behavioural changes observed (e.g., reduction in waste, increased diversity awareness)

Cautions

- Ensure that content is tailored to different job roles and contexts
- Make training engaging and avoid lecturing; use interactive and experiential elements
- Maintain momentum by integrating sustainability topics into ongoing communications and events

Glossary of terms

ADKAR Model

A goal-oriented change management model to guide individual and organizational change. It is an acronym for **Awareness**, **Desire**, **Knowledge**, **Ability**, and **Reinforcement**.

AI (Artificial Intelligence)

The simulation of human intelligence in machines, particularly computer systems. In the context of this book, it refers to tools like ChatGPT, Claude, and others that can generate text, analyze data, and perform tasks that typically require human cognition.

Balanced Scorecard

A strategic planning and management system used to align business activities to the vision and strategy of the organization, improve internal and external communications, and monitor organization performance against strategic goals. It balances financial measures with performance measures on customer, internal process, and learning/growth perspectives.

Blue Ocean Strategy

A business strategy that involves creating a new, uncontested market space ("Blue Ocean") rather than competing in an existing, saturated market ("Red Ocean"). It focuses on making the competition irrelevant by creating a leap in value for both the company and its buyers.

Business Model Canvas

A strategic management template for developing new or documenting existing business models. It is a visual chart with elements describing a firm's or product's value proposition, infrastructure, customers, and finances.

CMMS (Computerised Maintenance Management System)

Software that centralizes maintenance information and facilitates the processes of maintenance operations. It helps optimize the utilization and availability of physical equipment like vehicles, machinery, and communications infrastructure.

CRM (Customer Relationship Management)

A technology for managing all your company's relationships and interactions with customers and potential customers. The goal is simple: Improve business relationships to grow your business.

CSRD (Corporate Sustainability Reporting Directive)

An EU directive that requires companies to report on the impact of their activities on the environment and society, and on the business risks posed by sustainability issues. It aims to make sustainability reporting more common, consistent, and standardized.

Due Diligence

The investigation or exercise of care that a reasonable business or person is expected to take before entering into an agreement or contract with another party. In M&A, this involves a thorough review of the target company's financials, legal contracts, and operations.

EOQ (Economic Order Quantity)

The ideal order quantity a company should purchase to minimize inventory costs such as holding costs, shortage costs, and order costs.

ERP (Enterprise Resource Planning)

A type of software that organizations use to manage day-to-day business activities such as accounting, procurement, project management, risk management and compliance, and supply chain operations.

ESG (Environmental, Social, and Governance)

A framework used to assess an organization's business practices and performance on various sustainability and ethical issues. **Environmental** criteria consider how a company performs as a steward of nature. **Social** criteria examine how it manages relationships with employees, suppliers, customers, and the communities where it operates. **Governance** deals with a company's leadership, executive pay, audits, internal controls, and shareholder rights.

FRED (Federal Reserve Economic Data)

An online database consisting of hundreds of thousands of economic data time series from scores of national, international, public, and private sources, maintained by the Federal Reserve Bank of St. Louis.

Gantt Chart

A type of bar chart that illustrates a project schedule. It lists the tasks to be performed on the vertical axis, and time intervals on the horizontal axis. The width of the horizontal bars in the graph shows the duration of each activity.

GDPR (General Data Protection Regulation)

A regulation in EU law on data protection and privacy in the European Union and the European Economic Area. It also addresses the transfer of personal data outside the EU and EEA areas.

GHG (Greenhouse Gas) Protocol

The most widely used international accounting tool for government and business leaders to understand, quantify, and manage greenhouse gas emissions.

GRI (Global Reporting Initiative)

An international independent standards organization that helps businesses, governments and other organizations understand and communicate their impacts on issues such as climate change, human rights and corruption.

IRR (Internal Rate of Return)

A metric used in financial analysis to estimate the profitability of potential investments. It is a discount rate that makes the net present value (NPV) of all cash flows equal to zero in a discounted cash flow analysis.

ISO 27001

An international standard on how to manage information security. It details requirements for establishing, implementing, maintaining and continually improving an information security management system (ISMS).

K-means Clustering

A method of vector quantization, originally from signal processing, that aims to partition n observations into k clusters in which each observation belongs to the cluster with the nearest mean (cluster centroid).

KPI (Key Performance Indicator)

A quantifiable measure of performance over time for a specific objective. KPIs provide targets for teams to shoot for, milestones to gauge progress, and insights that help people across the organization make better decisions.

Lean Six Sigma

A method that relies on a collaborative team effort to improve performance by systematically removing waste and reducing variation. It combines the principles of Lean (eliminating waste) and Six Sigma (reducing defects) to improve efficiency and quality.

M&A (Mergers and Acquisitions)

A general term that describes the consolidation of companies or assets through various types of financial transactions, including mergers, acquisitions, consolidations, tender offers, purchase of assets and management acquisitions.

Materiality Assessment

The process of identifying and prioritizing the most significant environmental, social, and governance (ESG) issues for a company and its stakeholders.

Monte Carlo Simulation

A computerized mathematical technique that allows people to account for risk in quantitative analysis and decision making. It furnishes the decision-maker with a range of possible outcomes and the probabilities they will occur for any choice of action.

NIST (National Institute of Standards and Technology)

A non-regulatory agency of the United States Department of Commerce. Its mission is to promote innovation and industrial competitiveness. It develops cybersecurity standards, guidelines, and best practices.

NPS (Net Promoter Score)

A market research metric that is based on a single survey question asking respondents to rate the likelihood that they would recommend a company, product, or a service to a friend or colleague. It is used to gauge customer loyalty and satisfaction.

NPV (Net Present Value)

The difference between the present value of cash inflows and the present value of cash outflows over a period of time. NPV is used in capital budgeting and investment planning to analyze the profitability of a projected investment or project.

Pareto Chart

A type of chart that contains both bars and a line graph, where individual values are represented in descending order by bars, and the cumulative total is represented by the line. It is used to identify the most significant factors in a set of data.

RFP (Request for Proposal)

A business document that announces a project, describes it, and solicits bids from qualified contractors to complete it.

ROI (Return on Investment)

A performance measure used to evaluate the efficiency or profitability of an investment or compare the efficiency of a number of different investments. ROI measures the amount of return on a particular investment, relative to the investment's cost.

RPA (Robotic Process Automation)

A form of business process automation technology based on metaphorical software robots (bots) or artificial intelligence (AI) workers. It is used to automate repetitive, rules-based digital tasks.

SASB (Sustainability Accounting Standards Board)

An organization that provides sustainability accounting standards for publicly-listed companies. The standards are designed to help companies disclose financially-material sustainability information to investors.

SEC (U.S. Securities and Exchange Commission)

A large independent agency of the United States federal government, created to protect investors, maintain fair, orderly, and efficient markets, and facilitate capital formation.

SEO (Search Engine Optimization)

The process of improving the quality and quantity of website traffic to a website or a web page from search engines. SEO targets unpaid traffic rather than direct traffic or paid traffic.

SFDR (Sustainable Finance Disclosure Regulation)

An EU regulation that aims to increase transparency on how financial market participants and financial advisers integrate sustainability risks and consider adverse sustainability impacts in their processes.

SOX (Sarbanes-Oxley Act)

A U.S. federal law that mandates certain practices in financial record keeping and reporting for public companies to protect investors from fraudulent financial reporting by corporations.

SWOT Analysis

A strategic planning technique used to help a person or organization identify **Strengths**, **Weaknesses**, **Opportunities**, and **Threats** related to business competition or project planning.

TCFD (Task Force on Climate-related Financial Disclosures)

An organization established to develop recommendations for more effective climate-related disclosures that could promote more informed investment, credit, and insurance underwriting decisions.

Theory of Constraints

A management paradigm that views any manageable system as being limited in achieving more of its goals by a very small number of constraints. It focuses on identifying and managing these bottlenecks to improve overall throughput.

Joe Houghton

Business Consulting –
www.houghton.consulting

Joe is the owner of Houghton Consulting and offers a variety of consulting and training services via his website at www.houghton.consulting

Joe's **Project Management training** complements his being an Assistant Professor at the world-renowned UCD Smurfit Graduate School of Business. Joe established the MSc in Project Management at Smurfit back in 2005, and has been Academic Director of the programme since, growing it to now a full-time 1-year programme with 70 students each year and then also as an online, 2-year part-time programme with around 50 students across the 2 cohorts.

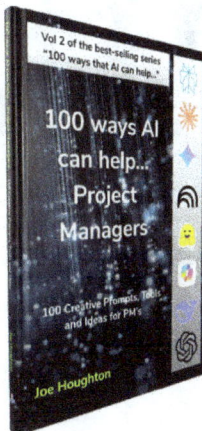

Joe has published a PM textbook – **"Project Management made easy...: the ECCSR approach"** – Amazon link https://amzn.to/3W0utAE and the 2nd book in this series **"100 ways AI can help... Project Managers"** – Amazon link - https://amzn.to/4n3Yx9v .

Artificial Intelligence plays to Joe's inner nerd – his early career was a a programmer and analyst and the applied tech side of computing has been a central fascination throughout his whole career. Constantly experimenting and using all the main AI tools, Joe now trains corporates, Govt departments, non-profits and educational institutions every week in this fast-moving space. He is an AI adviser to University College Dublin, The Institute of Bankers, and the Royal Photographic Society.

He has authored a number of books on AI primarily in the education space, all available on Amazon via his author page at https://www.amazon.co.uk/stores/Joe-Houghton/author/B07XWQRNJQ?ref=ap_rdr&isDramIntegrated=true&shoppingPortalEnabled=true :

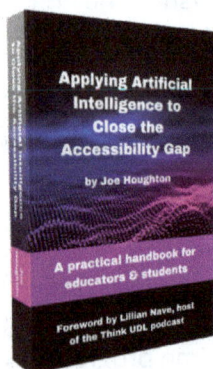

Contact Joe at joe.houghton@gmail.com to discuss any training needs you might have – always happy to discuss new opportunities!

Photography - www.houghtonphoto.com

Talks & Judging
Find all Joe's talk & judging details here - More than 20 talks / workshops and more in preparation! And I can always create a new talk - tell me what you would like...

Photography courses
Talk/workshop series - email or call Joe to discuss running these for your club!

Books by Joe Houghton
Streets of Dublin - a personal journey into street photography. Take your time - the art & craft of long exposure photography. Picture perfect - a beginner's guide to photography. And more in preparation...

1-1 tuition / coaching
Zoom or in-person photographic tuition - camera technique, post-processing, preparing for a distinction, backups & organising your images...Joe can help!

Joe Houghton has written 7 Amazon best-selling books on photography and delivered more than 1,200 talks to camera clubs and photographic societies around the world. He has judged at club, national and international level, and has more than 50 international salon acceptances.

Joe was Nikon's trainer in Ireland between 2003 & 2012 and has trained literally thousands of photographers from complete beginners through to seasoned professionals.
Joe is a regular contributor to the Royal Photographic Society where he delivers talks, workshops, articles to DIGIT and DI Online and acts as one of the RPS Digital Imaging Group's advisors on artificial intelligence.

His photography talks and books can all be accessed via his website at https://www.houghtonphoto.com/   Contact Joe at joe.houghton@gmail.com for talks, 1-1 online tuition or to discuss creating a new photographic learning experience for your group.

Books:

All Joe's photography books are available in hardback, paperback, on Kindle and also as audio books.

- **"Streets of Dublin: A street photography guide"** is available in 6" x 9" format on Amazon at https://amzn.to/3SsKDR2
- **"Take your time, the art and craft of long exposure photography"** is available in 6" x 9" format on Amazon at https://amzn.to/42mWhS1
- **"Picture perfect: A beginner's guide to photography"** is available in 6" x 9" format on Amazon at https://amzn.to/49nhsp5

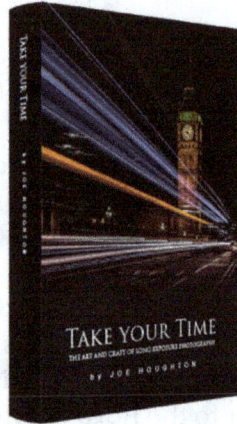

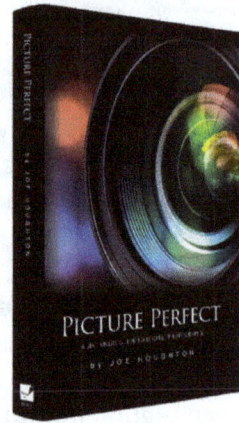

"Lightroom Classic Step by Step" is a 2 volume large format 8.5" x 11" set totalling over 700 pages that went straight to #1 & #2 in the Amazon photography manuals charts upon release in August 2025:

- Vol 1 – Organise & Find - on Amazon at https://amzn.to/4pJIJv6
- Vol 2 – Develop & Create – on Amazon at https://amzn.to/42cHhHB

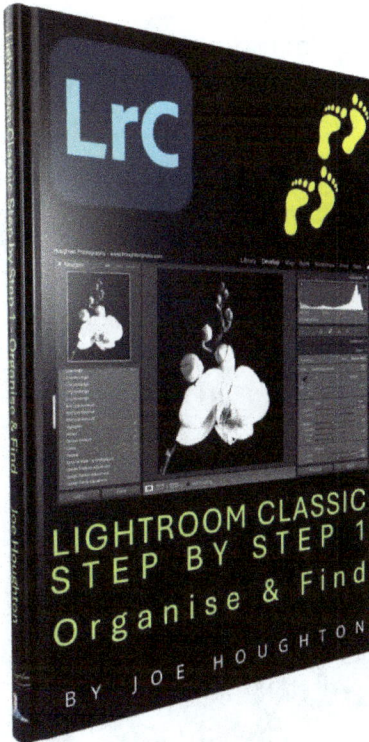

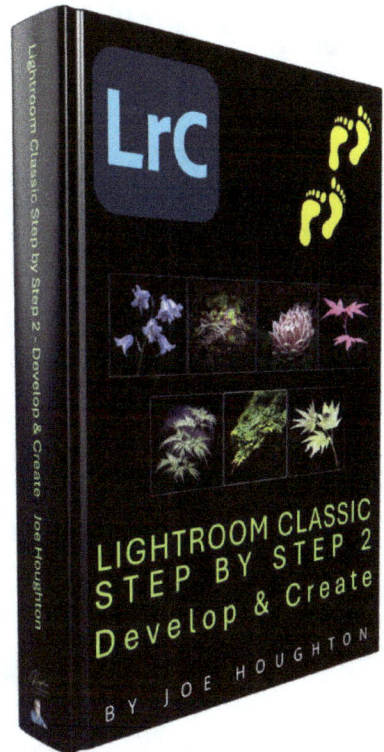

"Let's Shoot & Edit - Vol 1" is a 6"x9" format best-seller that also reached #1 in Amazon's photography books on release.
Amazon.co.uk link - https://amzn.to/4nV62QY

It covers the following topics:

- Mono
- Landscape
- Street
- Nature
- Portraits

- Flowers
- Abstract & ICM
- Long exposure
- Night
- Macro & close up

- Each topic is structured in a similar manner:
- Thing to consider pre-shoot
- Things to do during the shoot
- Post-processing tips and ideas
- Examples of top photographers in this area
- Some links to other resources – books, podcasts & websites

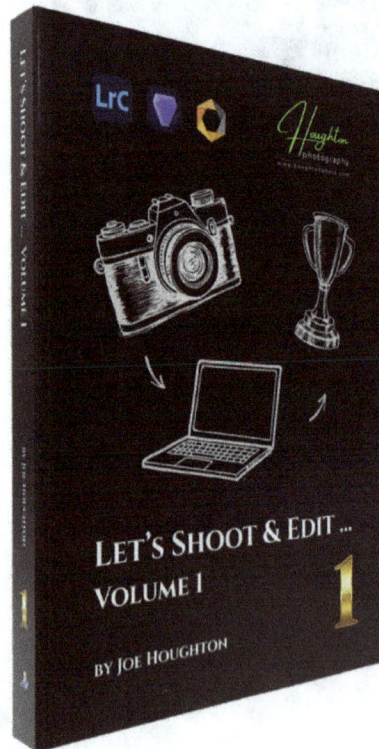

Index

www.ingramcontent.com/pod-product-compliance
Lightning Source LLC
Chambersburg PA
CBHW061155220326
41599CB00025B/4491